Taylor
October 1976

The Pro-Read Option Attack
For Winning Football

The Pro-Read Option Attack For Winning Football

STEVE AXMAN

Parker Publishing Company, Inc.   *West Nyack, N.Y.*

© 1976, by

PARKER PUBLISHING COMPANY, INC.

West Nyack, N.Y.

Library of Congress Cataloging in Publication Data

Axman, Steve
    The pro-read option attack for winning football.

    Includes index.
    1. Football--Offense. 2. Football coaching.
I. Title.
GV951.8.A95   796.33'22   76-5405
ISBN 0-13-731570-8

Printed in the United States of America

DEDICATION

To my wife, Marie
To my Mom & Dad, Mr. & Mrs. J. O. Axman
To my brother, Doug
To my buddy, Howard Vogts

How This Book Will Help You Control and Exploit Defenses

The Pro-Read Option Attack is an explosive offense that relies on a concept called defense-control to take what the defense gives the offense and to exploit the defense's weaknesses. It is option football of a different nature. Rather than the run-pitch option, the Pro-Read Option Attack is based on passing options that are built into the pass patterns. Today's offensive trend is the option; however, the trend in today's defenses is geared to the run-pitch option. Whether the I, veer or wishbone, the run-pitch option teams are facing eight- and even nine-man fronts through tightened defensive fronts and cheated-up secondaries. Common sense would dictate pass and not the run-pitch option. The Pro-Read Option Attack says option—but through the air.

The Pro-Read Option Attack is exacting, precise and relies on a limited number of simple, but explosive, plays. Instead of the run-pitch plays, it uses a few, explosive pass option patterns with receiver and passing options to attack any and all coverages. Blitzes, stunts, inverts, rolls, three deep, four deep—it doesn't matter since the execution of each pattern has built-in mechanisms to adjust to any and all defensive movement to exploit the defense through defense-control.

The Pro-Read Option Attack is based on simplicity of understanding and execution. Such simplicity allows for a minimum of mental errors and a maximum degree of efficiency. The run game is based on simple, quick hitting plays that rely on speed and execution—not "razzle-dazzle." The quick hitting run plays are aided in their effectiveness by the dictation of spread out defensive coverage by the passing game which loosens the defensive fronts, gives each defender a greater area to cover and lengthens the pursuit distances. The passing game uses only eleven pass patterns based on repetitive and easy-to-understand skills. Even the quarterback reads have been translated into a step-by-step pattern of play that is easy to understand and to teach. However, the sophistication and technical nature of the passing attack becomes a puzzling problem for the defense.

The Pro-Read Option Attack enables you to win with average talent. The offense enables you to utilize explosively those small speedsters too small for other offenses. It cuts down on the need for having two tight ends—perhaps the hardest position on the field to fill due to the stiff requirements of size, speed, toughness, blocking and catching ability —since the Pro-Read Option Attack only uses one tight end. It cuts down on the necessity of having three top-flight runners since the offense only utilizes one fullback-type and one halfback-type. The Pro-Read Option Attack even makes use of the heavier, but less muscular, linemen through the use of position pass blocking—a task far easier than digging out a defensive lineman from a hole!

Perhaps the Pro-Read Option Attack's best characteristic is its explosiveness. It is an offense that can score at any time from anywhere on the field, strike back quickly and pull a game "out of the fire" down to the last second of play. It is an exciting offense that enables the players to identify with the offenses of pro football itself. It is a great offensive strategy that instills within the players a sense of confidence that their offense cannot be stopped. The operation of the offense in itself instills player enthusiasm by the fact that it is challenging and fun both to practice and to play.

The Pro-Read Option Attack is a perfectly balanced offense that prevents the defense from overloading against any one particular aspect of the offense. It can attack inside, outside or through the air with equal efficiency. The balance between the run game and the pass game is smoothly integrated by play action passes, screens and draws developed directly from the running and passing plays. The Pro-Read Option Attack is also a consistent offense which can be used year after year. It has the flexibility to adapt to specific needs, talents and situations. In addition, it allows for a fluid progression of teaching continuity within the total program—from junior high on up. It is an offense that allows for a simplified introduction to basic offensive skills at the earliest stage of the feeder system, thereby creating the proper progression of skill development as players approach the varsity level.

By the technical nature of the pass patterns and their operation, the Pro-Read Option Attack combats the two things that can go wrong when you pass the ball. The offense utilizes defense-control by giving the receivers options as to where they can break their cuts to free themselves and get into open areas. It has the quarterback reading linebacker movements to prevent, or check, blitzing by use of the dump system. The wide receivers dictate coverages by the spreading out of the defense. In short, the Pro-Read Option Attack controls the defense and prevents it from attacking the offense while allowing the offense, instead, to attack the defense—defense control! It is not a gambling offense. The Pro-Read Option Attack is a sound ball-control offense in which we know to whom we are throwing and why.

The Pro-Read Option Attack shows that you need not fear not having a great, rifle-armed quarterback. Instead, it shows you how to take a good athlete and develop him into the leader of an explosive offensive machine. The book even tells you how to combat the rain, supposedly a common enemy of a passing attack, by turning the wet conditions into an extra offensive weapon.

This book is a detailed description of the offense—from selecting personnel to checking the blitz to practice drills. It presents an in-depth explanation of all the how's and why's that make the Pro-Read Option Attack an effective defense control that produces an explosive, exciting and highly motivating offensive system.

Steve Axman

ACKNOWLEDGEMENTS

We often hear how coaches beg, borrow and steal. Often, our greatest claims to originality are adaptations or modifications of others' ideas to fit our particular needs. This concept is quite true in the formation of the Pro-Read Option Attack and in the writing of this book. I would be quite remiss if I were not to mention that the passing theories of the Pro-Read Option Attack are based on many of the passing theories of C. W. Post College on Long Island. Under Head Coach Dom Anile, Post has developed into an eastern small-college powerhouse ranking nationally in passing almost every year. Actually, my ability to write this book is largely a result of the generosity of Coach Anile and his staff—their unselfish attitude and willingness to help the high school coach. The contributions to Long Island high school football alone have been both numerous and great. Very special thanks goes to C. W. Post's Passing Coordinator, Joe Terelli, who spent so much time helping me to understand many of the passing concepts presented in this book. Joe is an excellent coach with a tremendous knowledge of the passing game; I doubt if I could have found a better teacher.

Another person who has had much to do with my understanding of the passing concepts presented in this book is my good friend and ex-coaching rival, Jim Brennan, of Glen Cove High School, Glen Cove, L.I. Jim and I have worked together hours on end trying to perfect the Pro-Read Option passing concepts for simplified and effective high school use. I am also grateful for his review of the manuscript and his many helpful suggestions. I must also give special thanks to Coach Howard Vogts of Bethpage High School, Bethpage, L.I. Coach Vogts had the confidence in me to allow me to develop and experiment with the Pro-Read Option concepts while I was his assistant at Bethpage. Thanks also go to Mike Metzler, Quarterback Coach at East Stroudsburg State College, for his review of parts of the manuscript and to Maryanne Westly for her efforts in typing the manuscript.

S.A.

Contents

Defense Control Through the
Pro-Read Option Attack

The Pro-Read Option offense is more than the use of a pro set formation, utilizing a flanker and a split end. There are coaches who claim to use a pro set offense because their formation calls for two wide receivers. Their rationale for splitting two offensive players is to loosen the defensive front by forcing some kind of walk-away or cornerback coverage on the wide receivers. In practice, this is the initial theory of our Pro-Read Option offense. However, a pro set formation does not become a pro set or pro passing offense until the actual nature of the passing game can force such walk-away or cornerback coverage to cover the short passing game to the wide receivers.

In addition, the nature of the passing game must be able to dictate at least three-deep coverage of the secondary so that such short passing to the wide receivers cannot be covered by the secondary. The defense must be forced to use at least a three-deep coverage through the constant "home run" or "bomb" threat to the wide receivers. The mere presence of two wide receivers is not enough of a threat to dictate such walk-away or cornerback coverage to loosen the defensive front. One of the prime defensive rules is not to make major adjustments to wide receiver splits in the short passing zones until successes of the offense force us to do so. Far too often receivers are split out as decoys in an effort to spread the defense and to help open up the running game. The offense becomes little more than a running offense with two split receivers. A coach may be able to "hide" weak personnel at these wide receiver positions since he has little intention of using them while still successfully spreading the defense.

THE PRO-READ OPTION OFFENSE

The Pro-Read Option offense is a well-balanced ball control offense that utilizes a concept called defense-control to attack various defenses that are faced. Defense-control means that a team can exploit the weaknesses of another team's defense. Such defense-control is made possible by the nature of the offensive formation, the drop-back passing series, running game and complementary play action, and draw and screen series. The defense-control is achieved through the application of the seven basic theories of the Pro-Read Option offense. The major emphasis of the offensive theories stems from the design of the drop-back pro passing series—the basis of the offense for which it is named.

1. SPREAD THE DEFENSE

The primary concern is to spread the defense by use of the drop-back passing series to prevent the defense from having the ability to utilize eight-, nine- and sometimes even seven-man fronts. Such a spreading of the defense and prevention of an eight- or nine-man front is accomplished by forcing the defense to utilize walk-away or cornerback coverages against the wide receivers by using Max-In and Max-Out patterns. The quarterback's initial assignment, once he lines up at the line of scrimmage, is to check for walk-away or cornerback coverage, called "coverage-and-a-half." If the defense is in a tight eight- or nine-man front leaving the short flat and hook zones open, he uses an audible to check off the huddle play call and instead calls for a Max-In pattern. See Diagram 1-1.

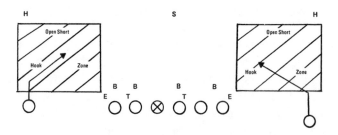

Diagram 1-1
Max-In Cut Threat to Force Coverage-and-a-Half

The defense may try to compensate for the success of the Max-In cut by putting the outside linebacker in a switched position just off the defensive end. If such a switched alignment occurs, the Max-Out pattern is called and the open short flat zone exploited. Such Max-Out patterns are also called if the defense tries to compensate for the Max-In pattern by using an inverted defensive halfback alignment, as shown in Diagram 1-2.

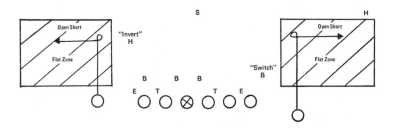

Diagram 1-2
Max-Out Cut Threat to Force Coverage-and-a-Half

If the defense tries to compensate for the Max-Out pattern by bringing up the outside deep back, the quarterback arm pumps the wide receiver on his out cut, signaling the wide receiver to "bust-up" the sideline past the forcing deep back to receive the "T.D. bomb" pass. See Diagram 1-3.

Diagram 1-3
Pump-up of Wide Receiver on Max-Out Cuts
To Force Coverage-and-a-Half

The use of the Max-In and -Out cuts to spread the defense by forcing coverage-and-a-half accomplishes two major goals. The weakened (in number and strength) defensive front opens the running game, and the defense must sacrifice run support in an effort to strengthen pass defense.

Secondly, due to such forcing of coverage-and-a-half, the defense cannot rush more than seven men. This is of great importance to the drop-back passing series since the design of the passing patterns enables the offense to block or check the rushes of seven men. This is accomplished through use of the marriage pass blocking scheme and the dump pass system (use of "hot" receivers), to check blitzing linebackers. In turn, the failure to rush more than seven men enables the offense to utilize the five-man pass patterns of the drop-back passing series.

With an odd-numbered front and four-man secondaries, double cornerback defenses are usually used. However, a team rarely can force double walk-away coverage against eight-man fronts utilizing three-deep secondaries. Few teams allow an uncovered tight end in a pro set formation; therefore, walk-away coverage to the flanker side rarely occurs versus such defenses. In addition, many coaches feel they are able to cover the Max-In cut of the flanker with the flat zone pass coverage of the tight end linebacker. If walk-away coverage is given to the tight end and flanker side, the run game to the tight end side is wide open. If no walk-away coverage is given, the goal of limiting the defense to a seven-man front by forcing such coverage to the split end side is still achieved. In addition, the open short passing zones to the flanker side can be exploited at opportune times. By not continually exploiting the short passing zones to the flanker side, a team can set up throwing to such cuts on crucial situations by lulling the tight end side linebacker into the false sense of security that his flat pass responsibility is not of immediate concern. The team is also balanced to the tight end side by having the extra blocker in the form of the tight end. Thus, the outside linebacker over the tight end is checked by the blocking of the tight end on the run and, as will be seen, checked by the dump system on a pass if he attempts to blitz.

2. CONTROL BLITZING LINEBACKERS

The "Read" portion of the Pro-Read Option offense deals with the reading of the defensive alignments before the ball is snapped and movements of the defense after the ball is snapped. The reading of the defensive alignment by the quarterback, in an effort to force the defense to use a seven-man front or less, is an example reading of alignment. Other reading of alignment is discussed in Chapter 4. The reading of defensive movements after the ball is snapped involves two facets—the reading of linebacker movement and the reading of secondary movement.

The reading of linebacker movement by the quarterback, backs and tight end is actually all part of the second theory of the Pro-Read Option offense—control blitzing linebackers. The most serious threat our offense faces is the blitz. As previously mentioned, the forcing of coverage-and-a-half or cornerback coverage limits the possible rush to seven men. Thus, the possibility of an eight-man rush through blitzing is checked, and the combination of a marriage pass blocking and dump pass system checks a seven-man rush. The dump, or "hot" receiver system has the offensive quarterback, tight end and backs reading the initial movements of certain linebackers. If blitz occurs, the "hot" receivers are read to see which receiver has been left open to receive the "dump" ball via a quick pop type of pass. The basis of the theory is that a blitzing linebacker must cause the defense to vacate, or leave open, a short passing zone. The passing patterns and blocking system enable the offense either to block everyone in a seven-man rush or to control linebacker blitzing by using automatic dump passes to designated receivers. Furthermore, defense-control is insured by exploiting what the defense has revealed.

3. CONTROL MAN-TO-MAN PASS COVERAGES

The third theory of the offense deals with controlling man-to-man pass coverages, accomplished by using isolating and crossing pass patterns. If a receiver is played in a tight man-to-man technique, isolating pass patterns should be used to pit the receivers against one-on-one pass coverage. Such isolation fully allows the receivers to take advantage of cut options—one of which allows the receivers to bust up deep on converging man-to-man coverage in an effort to streak past such coverage. The other option for the receiver is to adjust his cut to stay under zone coverage. This is discussed in the next theory.

The use of crossing pass patterns is another method of controlling man-to-man coverage. Actually, this is also an isolation technique in which deep backs are forced to cover receivers breaking away from them rather than into their area. An excellent example of this, shown in Diagram 1-4, is an isolation of a deep sideline out pattern by a tight end against a strong safety in a man-to-man technique.

4. CONTROL ZONE PASS COVERAGES

The fourth major concern is controlling zone pass coverages, accomplished either by throwing underneath the deep zone of the secondary between the deep backs and the linebackers or by flooding a zone with an overload of receivers. The reading technique is utilized when throwing

Diagram 1-4
Crossing Pattern Vs. Man-to-Man Coverage

under the zone by use of the cut options. Contrary to the read of man-to-man coverage, the receivers do not bust deep. Instead, once they read zone coverage they cut back to the quarterback on a comeback technique by breaking post, flag, fly and deep cuts into hook-up cuts. Thus, the receiver's cut ends up between the deep zone of the secondary and the short pass zone drop of the linebackers.

In both the control of man-to-man and zone pass coverages, the "read" portion of the Pro-Read Option offense is enacted. Such reading allows the offense to maintain defense-control by taking advantage of what the defense leaves open. All reading of the Pro-Read Option offense is simplified by the fact that only one basic formation is used—a pro right with the flanker right and the split end left. By showing a consistent formation, the offense finds that the defense also shows a consistent tendency to declare its formations early, adjustments and all. Also, the quarterback and receivers have an easier time spotting the alignment and its keys.

5. CONTROL THE WEAKENED DEFENSIVE FRONT INSIDE

Another reason for trying to force coverage-and-a-half or cornerback coverage to make sure that no more than a seven-man front can be used is to open up the running game. Simple reasoning is used: the less the number of people in the defensive front, the easier the blocking for the run game. Secondly, a spread out defense is not able to pursue as well as a tight defense since the players have greater distances to pursue. In addition, the personnel in the defensive front have greater defensive areas to cover.

The inside running game controls the weakened defensive front inside by attacking the defensive weaknesses. To accomplish this goal, the offense uses an extremely quick hitting power and counter series. Since the spread-out defense cannot pursue well, the offense can open holes quickly in its front and bust our backs into the secondary by hitting the hole with maximum take-off speed on the line.

6. CONTROL THE WEAKENED DEFENSIVE FRONT OUTSIDE

The forcing of coverage-and-a-half or cornerback coverage has helped the outside running game greatly. To cover the Max-In and -Out cuts, the defenses are forced into such outside linebacker and cornerback adjustments. Thus, the corner of the defensive front has been spread out and greatly weakened. The corner or contain units now have more ground to cover and greater pursuit distance; they are concerned with immediate pass responsibilities and are forced out of the basic, and usually strongest, defensive formation. The sweep game is similar to the inside running game in that quick hitting of the corner by the blocking back and the ball carrier helps to exploit the defensive weaknesses. Thus, the running game as a whole makes use of defense-control to take advantage of defensive weaknesses.

7. BALANCE OFFENSE WITH PLAY ACTION, SCREEN AND DRAW SERIES

The final theory of the offense is to utilize effective play action, screen and draw series to create a total balance and coordination of the offense. These series help to create such complete coordination: screens and draws complement the passing game, the counter series complements the power and sweep series, and the play action pass series complements all three. Thus, any part of the game can be supplemented at any time. Keying strengths is extremely difficult since any overloading techniques by the defense can be counter-attacked.

2

Selecting Personnel for the Pro-Read Option Attack

The careful placement of personnel helps to balance the offense carefully and to utilize the talents of the available football players most effectively.

The Tackles: Referring to the left side of the line as the quick side rather than the weak side, avoids the derogatory description of a lineman as the *weak* guard or tackle. The left tackle and left guard must be the faster of the two tackles and guards because the left tackle faces many weak side defensive adjustments that see him blocking more linebackers than the right tackle. Thus, he must be large enough and strong enough to block defensive tackles. Yet, he must also have the quickness and agility to go after linebackers. As in all linemen, the tackles should have wide rear ends. These types of linemen have good balance because of a wide base and make excellent pass blockers. The tackles should be big, burly, aggressive linemen who enjoy going after people. Both tackles must be the type who enjoy the challenge of having the ball run over their holes since the off-tackle power is such a bread-and-butter play in our running game. Quickness and agility are also keys to sealing on a defensive tackle over the offensive guard when the guard is pulling.

The right tackle is usually the bigger, stronger and more aggressive tackle since most defenses beef up to the strong, tight end side anyway. Thus, the right tackle is often faced with the opposition's strongest and toughest defensive tackle or outside linebacker. The same is true when he must pass block the defensive end. Though large, he must still be mobile and agile enough to seal block for the guard when he pulls and to block linebackers when necessary.

Although the bigger and stronger tackle may be at the right tackle spot, this does not mean that the right tackle is the better tackle. As a matter of fact, the left tackle and left guard are the more complete and best linemen; they must be better athletes than the right side linemen. Because the defensive strength is stacked to our tight end side, the greatest successes in the running game are to the left side. For this reason, the running game is more left-handed than right-handed although a totally balanced attack is the goal. Thus, the best, or most complete, guards and tackles usually are found on the left side.

The Guards: These players are usually the best athletes among the offensive linemen. They must be tough enough and strong enough to block defensive tackles on run plays and in pass blocking, as well as quick and agile enough to pull to trap block, lead sweeps and block linebackers.

The key to guard play is quickness and agility. In the counter and sweep series they must pull, quickly get down the line of scrimmage to trap a tackle, kick out the secondary contain on a sweep or cut up inside of a kick out block of the defensive end to lead the sweep. Being able to read the lead back's block on the defensive end in the sweep and to adjust his pull route properly either inside the kickout block or around the hook block of the defensive end require great agility on the part of the guards. It is usually the lack of agility that prevents a player from handling the guard assignments.

The left guard, like the left tackle, must be the faster of the two guards since he has at least an extra yard to go to get around the block of the defensive end on the sweep when pulling. This, of course, is because the tight end is on the right side and thus, the defensive end is that much farther away from the left guard. Such a rationale may sound quite picayune; however, running plays are designed on split-second timing. A slower guard with an extra yard to travel may be just enough of a problem to cause the play to break down due to his inability to get to the blocking assignment in time. In the meantime, the slower guard can be more effective on the right side since his pulling left is to the short side of the formation where his distance to travel is less.

The Center: The characteristics of a good center are not often easy to find. Although these characteristics are probably closest to those of the left tackle, quickness and agility are more important than size and strength. He should be at least 5′10″ or better so that the quarterback does not have to bend down too low to get his hands under the center. The quarterback should be able to reach under the center and still stand as tall as possible with his back straight. If the center is too low, the quarterback has to bend over hunchback style, hindering his ability to read the defensive alignments.

The center must possess quickness and agility rather than brute strength and size since, for the most part, he is blocking noseguards or inside linebackers—positions which utilize quickness, penetration and pursuit. Rather than concentrating on driving out a large defensive lineman, the center should focus on an angling noseguard trying to penetrate a gap or an inside linebacker trying to flow to the ball.

The last important quality in a center is a peppery, fiery attitude. He is the mainstay of the line, its leader by alignment and play execution. He is responsible for forming the huddle, keeping its order, setting the line's alignment and the all-important delivery of the ball to the quarterback —this is all in addition to his blocking assignment. He must have a cocky, competitive attitude that radiates confidence and enthusiasm to the rest of the offense.

The Tight End: This player must be the best athlete on the offense, the most complete offensive football player. He must block as well as tackle, be fast and agile enough to carry the football, be tough enough to catch the ball in a crowd and have hands as good as any receiver. He should have good size, should be a very durable player who enjoys physical contact and must be able to break a big play with speed and good running ability. Since defensive coverages concentrate on wide receivers, the tight end is often the leading receiver at the end of the season. Thus, he must possess almost every desirable trait of a football player: size, toughness, aggressiveness, speed and agility.

The Wide Receivers: The split end and flanker do not require any particular size characteristics. The main qualities in wide receivers, or "burners," are speed and good hands. The greater their speed, the greater the success of the passing game since they pose such a great "home run" threat. Few defenses ever give up the deep threat. When a "burner" is split or flanked out wide, he usually dictates loosened coverage by the deep backs, increasing the success of offensive hook-up cuts off of the post and flag cuts since the open area under the zone is enlarged. Such a threat of speed even helps the running game because the deep backs cannot support the run quickly.

Basketball guards make great wide receivers. They usually have excellent quickness and hands, as well as good speed. Their fine athletic ability usually enables them to develop deceptive faking moves off of their cuts.

The last characteristic of wide receivers is toughness. Although size is not essential, he must be tough enough to hold onto the ball after he makes his catch, to catch in a crowd and not be afraid to throw a downfield block on a man in the secondary.

The Fullback: This player is in the category of the tight end, except that he need not be as adept a blocker. Actually, he is the typical fullback type: he should have good size and be a strong, dependable bread-and-butter type of runner who can get the tough, short yardage needed in crucial situations. He also must have good speed so that he can carry the ball around the left end on the sweep. For this reason, the fullback always lines up on the right side and the halfback on the left (except for the "I" set). Like the pulling right guard, the fullback has a shorter distance to go to turn the corner. The halfback, as the speedster in the backfield, is called upon to sweep around the longer right, or tight end, side. In the "I" set, the fullback has upback duties; thus, he must enjoy blocking. He also should be a good enough "daylight" runner to carry on the draw.

The fullback must be a good receiver who is not afraid to catch in a crowd; he has dump pass responsibilities as a "hot" receiver over the short hook zone area of the defense. He also must be tough enough to hang onto the ball when making a catch over the middle since he immediately receives punishment from the linebackers and deep backs.

The Halfback: Called the "speed merchant," the halfback is a game breaker with wide receiver speed and excellent running ability. As previously mentioned, he always lines up on the left, with the exception of the "I," to utilize his speed in turning the corner on the tight end side on the sweep. Speed, agility and elusiveness are his major desirable qualities. He must be tough enough to take punishment when he runs inside and must not be afraid to stick his nose into a blitzing linebacker on a pass block. He also should have good hands since he is often called upon to act as a receiver. Although he need not be the greatest of blockers, he cannot be afraid to throw a block. One of the major characteristics of both the halfback and the fullback is aggressiveness. If players have this quality, along with some speed, they can be taught the rest.

The Quarterback: Quarterbacks are made, not found. An intelligent young man approximately six feet tall with a strong arm and, most importantly, a winning instinct can develop into an excellent pro-type quarterback. There are dozens of strong-armed baseball and basketball players who meet these qualifications. Proper coaching and development can turn such players into fine passers and quarterbacks. It is form and follow-through that determine passing ability.

Being tall is a very helpful trait. The ability to read the defense and throw over the outstretched hands of the defensive linemen is greatly aided by such height. Although the quarterback need not be a genius, an intelligent player has greater insight into the operation of the offense and how it can be run effectively.

If the quarterback were to have only one of these desired traits, it should be his "winning instinct." There is no substitute for having a winner as quarterback. He may be small, not a great passer and not a genius; but a winner leads an offense into the end zone one way or another. Such a person has the confidence necessary to be a leader—a field general in the true sense of the term.

The Pro-Read Option quarterback does not run the ball in a run-pitch option series; thus, he need not be a great runner. He should be a fair enough runner to bootleg the ball occasionally and run a quarterback draw. If the quarterback is a good enough athlete, he can master all the quarterback skills of passing, running, ball handling and faking through desire, dedication and hard work.

3

Pro-Read Option Attack Nomenclature

SPLITS OF THE WIDE RECEIVERS

There are three basic rules for wide receivers which attempt to get them split approximately twelve yards from the last man on the line of scrimmage. If the ball is at midfield, the wide receivers split approximately three yards outside of the hashmark. See Diagram 3-1.

Diagram 3-1
Wide Receiver Splits With Ball At Midfield

When the ball is on the hashmark, the onside wide receiver splits no closer than four yards to the sideline. The offside receiver splits at least outside the far hashmark, as in Diagram 3-2.

On any out cuts by the wide receivers, the normal split should be cut down approximately two yards from twelve to ten yards. Such alignment, illustrated in Diagram 3-3, often puts the receiver inside the hashmark in an effort to create additional running room to execute the cut.

All alignments are approximate with respect to following the split

Diagram 3-2
Wide Receiver Splits With Ball On Hashmark

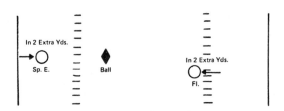

Diagram 3-3
Wide Receiver Splits On Out Cuts

rules. The wide receivers must use their discretion when splitting to consider if they are the prime receivers and whether or not they must vary their splits to prevent the defense from picking up keys.

BACKFIELD SETS

There are three backfield sets. The Blue set is the balanced set of the offense in relation to the alignment of the halfback left and the flanker right, with the fullback stacked behind the quarterback at a depth of four yards. The halfback aligns in the guard-tackle gap at a depth of three-and-one-half yards, as shown in Diagram 3-4.

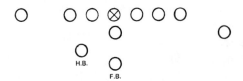

Diagram 3-4
Blue Set

The Red set, Diagram 3-5, is a split set. The halfback takes the same alignment and the fullback takes a similar guard-tackle gap alignment at a depth of three-and-one-half yards.

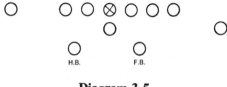

Diagram 3-5
Red Set

The "I" set places the fullback in an up-back position at three-and-one-half yards with the halfback taking a tailback position at four-and-one-half yards. See Diagram 3-6.

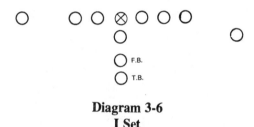

Diagram 3-6
I Set

HOLE NUMBERING

The system of numbering holes actually numbers the gaps between offensive linemen. All even-numbered holes are to the right, all odd-numbered holes to the left, as shown in Diagram 3-7.

The hole numbering is used only in the power series. An off-tight end power is not run since it is included as part of the sweep game. Therefore, the off-tight end hole is not numbered the eight hole.

Diagram 3-7
Hole Numbering

PLAY CALLING AND STARTING COUNT

All plays, except the power and the power play action passes, utilize descriptive word calls. Thus, a sweep left from the blue formation is called "Blue, Sweep Left." The call "on the first go" is added to signal on what "go" count the ball is to be snapped. When calling a power or play action pass off of the powers, the player must add the number of the hole he is either running at or faking to set up the play action pass. Thus, an "I, Power 1" is the call for running a tailback power with a fullback lead at the left guard-tackle gap from the I set.

The execution of the audible check-off play calling and starting count system at the line of scrimmage assumes the following order of execution:

1. "Hut":   This is the call to go on a quick count from an upright position before the set.

2. "Number" (3-8):   This call has the quarterback telling the offense how many defensive linemen there are and their approximate positions (explained in detail in Chapter 9).

3. "Color and Number" (1-5) } These calls are made once to each side
4. "Color and Number" (1-5) }   of the line.

                        They are the check-off audible calls. If the live color of the game is called, the next number tells what audible play will be used instead.

5. "Set":   This signals the line and backs to set and have the line make its line calls (explained in Chapter 6).

6. "Go" Call: This is the execution of the starting count given in the huddle.

If the live color of the game is called during the sequence of the calling, the play called in the huddle is canceled. Instead, the number following the live color tells what check-off play will be used. Four or five check-off calls are used in a game; they are as follows:

#1 =   Max-In pass pattern
#2 =   Max-Out pass pattern
#3 =   Max-Back pass pattern
#4 = } Special check-off plays for each particular game.
#5 = }

An example of the signal calling and audible check-off system for a game in which "Blue" is the live color is as follows:

"Hut, 4, Red 1, Red 1, Set, Go!" (The play called in the huddle is run on the first "go" since the live color was not used.)

"Hut, 4, Blue 3, Blue 3, Set, Go, Go!" (The live color is given so the play called in the huddle is canceled. Instead, the #3 check-off play—the "Max-Back" pass pattern—is used on the second "Go," the same starting count called in the huddle.)

4

Developing the Basics of the Drop-Back Passing Series

Chapter 1 develops the concept that all theories of the offense are based on the Drop-Back Passing Series. The use of the Max-In and Max-Out cut patterns to force coverage-and-a-half has been explained already. It is the purpose of this chapter to show how the Drop-Back Passing Series controls linebacker blitzing, man-to-man coverage and zone coverages

RECEIVER CUTS

Since descriptive terms are used to identify both the total pass pattern and the cuts in the pattern, numbers are unnecessary. This is an excellent aid to teaching the offense, and it greatly helps the instruction and understanding of an individual cut or route as part of the total design of the pass pattern. A Tight-Across cut tells the receiver what to do rather than having to remember that an 8 or a 9 cut is the Tight-Across cut.

Max-In Cut (Flanker and Split End)

One step burst off line of scrimmage and take approximately a 45° angle cut into the most open area of the short hook zone. Look for ball immediately on second step. See Diagram 4-1.

Diagram 4-1
Max-In Cut

Max-Out (Flanker and Split End)

Split end bursts off line of scrimmage for six steps, flanker for seven. On last step, shift weight to back portion of ball of foot so center of body gravity is over the outside leg. Throw back inside arm to help rotate body back toward the quarterback in an effort to take more than a 180° turn step with the inside foot. Take a cross-over step with the outside foot and look for the ball immediately while breaking to the sideline. See Diagram 4-2.

Diagram 4-2
Max-Out Cut

Max-Back (Flankers and Split Ends)

Burst off the line for fourteen yards in an effort to get the deep back to stay deep. Plant your inside foot, shifting weight to the back portion of the ball of the foot. Throw your outside elbow back to take a 135° angle cut back toward the sidelines. Look immediately for a low, hard pass at approximately twelve yards. This is a first down cut when short to medium distance yardage is needed. See Diagram 4-3.

Post Cut (Flankers and Split Ends)

Burst off line of scrimmage at top speed for twelve yards. Veer forward off hip of deep back in an effort to get him to turn his hips in the

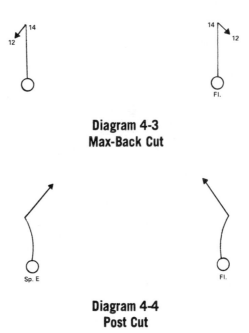

Diagram 4-3
Max-Back Cut

Diagram 4-4
Post Cut

opposite direction of final cut. This severely limits his ability to stay with you. (If deep back picks up this initial veer as a key, you can run straight at him or veer to the onside of your final cut and use a short jigger step to his offside as a fake.) Final cut is to goalposts. See Diagram 4-4.

Flag Cut (Flankers and Split Ends)

Run identically to Post Cut with exception of initial veer to inside and final cut to the sideline flag. See Diagram 4-5.

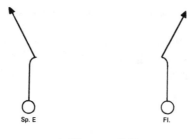

Diagram 4-5
Flag Cut

Across Cut (Flankers and Tight Ends)

Burst off line of scrimmage for seven to eight yards (eight to nine for the flanker), give a quick "jigger" step to the outside and cut across field to left on 90° angle. The tight end must initially step out laterally toward the sidelines, as well as vertically to bend up on an alley release. This is done so the tight end does not come too close to the fly cut of the fullback, allowing the fullback to clear out. See Diagram 4-6.

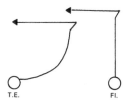

Diagram 4-6
Across Cut

Shute Cut (Tight Ends, Fullbacks and Halfbacks)

A 30° angle cut off the tight end area toward the short flat zone. The receiver looks for the ball immediately over his outside shoulder. See Diagram 4-7.

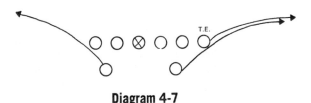

Diagram 4-7
Shute Cut

Fly (Alley-Fly) Cut (Tight Ends, Fullbacks and Halfbacks)

A simple streak cut in which the receiver is bursting deep as fast as possible in an effort to beat the deep backs deep or to clear out the deep zone area under the deep backs. All three receivers may be given alley-fly cuts in which they must take off laterally as well as vertically so that the fly cut can be executed through the short hook zone alley. See Diagram 4-8.

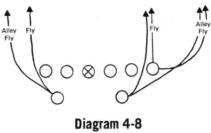

Diagram 4-8
Alley Cuts

Tight-Delay Cut (Tight End only)

The tight end blocks out on the defensive end for two counts, turns to the inside facing the quarterback and takes a crossfield direction underneath the linebacker drops. See Diagram 4-9.

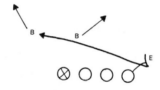

Diagram 4-9
Tight-Delay Cut

Tight-Deep Cut (Tight End only)

The tight end bursts off the line of scrimmage as fast as possible on a fly type of cut for five steps. On the fifth step he plants his outside (right) foot and cuts right at the safety (strong safety in a four deep). He takes

Diagram 4-10
Tight-Deep Cut

three steps directly at the safety and stares directly into his eyes in an attempt to freeze the safety. A "freeze" means putting the safety into a sweat where he must freeze or stop his movement in an effort to determine what the tight end is doing. On the tight end's third step he plants his left foot and breaks on a 90° angle to his right for the flag, looking for the ball immediately over his outside shoulder. See Diagram 4-10.

Tight-Out Cut (Tight End only)

The tight-out cut is identical to the across pattern with the exception that the tight end fakes to the inside and breaks to the sideline. Once he makes his out cut he must read the coverage of the deep back and the flat coverage to determine which area is most open for him to bend his cut into. See Diagram 4-11.

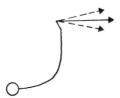

Diagram 4-11
Tight-Out Cut

Hook Cut (Fullback only)

This is a simple hook-in maneuver off of a fly cut into the most open area of the middle short passing zone. The cut is run by the fullback through the left guard, left tackle area. The hook is at a depth of twelve to fourteen yards. See Diagram 4-12.

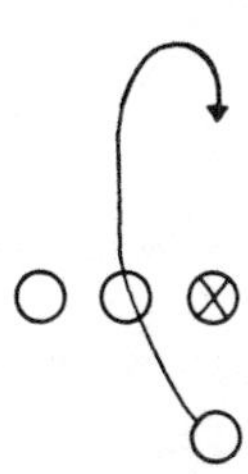

Diagram 4-12
Hook Cut

Deep Cut (Fullback and Tight End)

This is a deep bend up cut behind the weak safety or the offside defensive halfback in an effort to occupy him on a man-to-man or rotated zone coverage. If the deep back fails to pick the deep cut up, the receiver continues to bust up deep looking up for the ball. See Diagram 4-13.

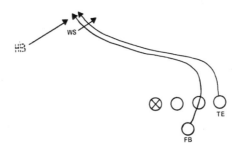

Diagram 4-13
Deep Cut

Flare Cut (Halfback only)

The halfback breaks to the left sideline for three steps and bends up on a 45° angle arc, looking immediately inside for the ball. The halfback is a safety valve receiver on this cut as it is only used in one pattern—the Max-In. See Diagram 4-14.

Diagram 4-14
Flare Cut

THE DUMP PASS SYSTEM

On the start of every pass pattern in the drop-back series, with the exception of the Max patterns, the movements of certain linebackers are read to see if a blitz occurs or a short passing zone is left open (vacated). If the read shows blitz or vacated short passing zone, the assigned "hot" receiver is checked to see if a dump pass is open to him. The "hot" receiver is the tight end or one of the backs, depending on the pattern being run.

On all drop-back patterns, again with the exception of the Max patterns, the quarterback and the Mike-Hot receiver check the movement of the Mike linebacker, the first linebacker on or to the right of the center on his first two steps. See Diagram 4-15.

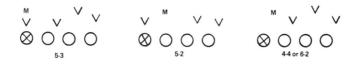

Diagram 4-15
The Mike Read of Various Defenses

The Mike-Hot receiver is either the tight end or the fullback, depending on the pattern called. If the Mike linebacker blitzes or vacates his short hook zone by covering another short pass zone instead, the Mike-Hot receiver calls out "Hot" to the quarterback and looks for a quick dump pass to be thrown to him. The Mike-Hot receiver bends into the open short hook zone area. The quarterback reads the movement of the Mike linebacker and if he reads "blitz" or "vacate," he checks to see if the Mike-Hot receiver is open to receive a dump pass. If the Mike read dictates "dump" (open Mike-Hot receiver), the rest of the pass pattern is canceled and the short seven-to-ten-yards dump pass gain is achieved. Such successive pass completions help to insure ball control while also controlling the blitz. The only time it may not be wise to settle for the sure short gain is if a team is down two or more touchdowns late in the game and is forced to go for the longer gain. See Diagram 4-16.

If the Mike linebacker drops to his hook zone, the Mike-Hot receiver continues on his designated route, and the quarterback looks to his second dump read if the pattern called has a second assignment. If there is no second dump read, the quarterback takes his full eight-step drop and completes the normal pass pattern. This continuation of the pass pattern is also executed if the Mike read dictates "dump," but the Mike-Hot receiver shows "color." In this case, "color" refers to the fact that no dump pass is thrown to a "hot" receiver if the quarterback sees an opposite color jersey covering the "hot" receiver or receivers as shown in Diagram 4-17. The quarterback instead either checks his second dump read, if he has one, or completes an eight-step drop and continues the

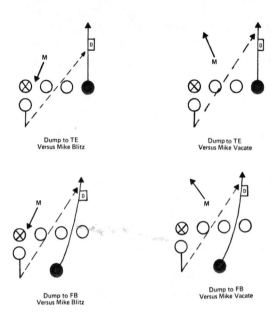

Dump to TE
Versus Mike Blitz

Dump to TE
Versus Mike Vacate

Dump to FB
Versus Mike Blitz

Dump to FB
Versus Mike Vacate

Diagram 4-16
Mike-Hot Dump Reads

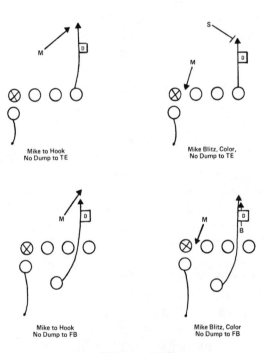

Mike to Hook
No Dump to TE

Mike Blitz, Color,
No Dump to TE

Mike to Hook
No Dump to FB

Mike Blitz, Color
No Dump to FB

Diagram 4-17
Mike Reads—No Dumps

normal pass pattern assignments. "Color" usually occurs when a deep back "jumps" on a "hot" receiver to cover for a stunting or blitzing linebacker. Three- and four-deep roll coverages also can produce such "color."

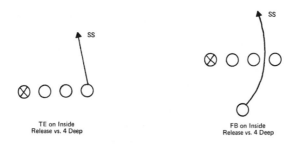

TE on Inside
Release vs. 4 Deep

FB on Inside
Release vs. 4 Deep

Diagram 4-18
Mike-Hot Receiver Release Vs. 4 Deep

The release of the Mike-Hot receiver is important to the effective execution of his designated role in the pass pattern. This release directly correlates to the alignment of the safety, who is in the best position to nullify the effectiveness of his dump responsibilities. A simple rule is used: versus a four-deep secondary, the tight end or fullback takes an inside release (inside of the strong safety) to position himself between the strong safety and the ball. In effect, he screens the strong safety out with his back aiding his ability to receive a dump pass. See Diagram 4-18.

Versus a three-deep secondary, the Mike-Hot receiver takes an outside release in an effort to stay as far away from the safety as possible. The safety, basically aligned in centerfield of the deep secondary, cannot cover a widened Mike-Hot release that is practically splitting the seam in between the safety and the right defensive halfback. See Diagram 4-19.

As soon as the tight end takes his alignment at the line of scrimmage, he is responsible for checking the secondary. He calls out a "three" or a "four" to alert all receivers as to whether the coverage is three or four deep. This, in turn, alerts the Mike-Hot receiver to take an inside or outside release.

In all Flanker and Tight End patterns, with the exception of the Tight-Delay pattern, there is a second dump read to the tight end (right) side of the pro set formation. All explanations of the Mike and Blood reads are shown from the Red (split) set as all Flanker and Tight End pass patterns are run from the Red set. The second read is on the second

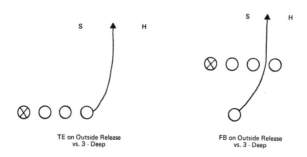

Diagram 4-19
Mike-Hot Receiver Release Vs. 3 Deep

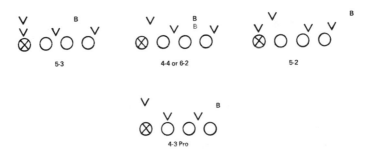

Diagram 4-20
The Blood Read of Various Defenses

linebacker to the right side of the center, called the Blood linebacker. Against four deep secondaries or defenses utilizing outside lineback coverages the Blood read is on the outside linebacker or cornerback. See Diagram 4-20.

The Blood-Hot receiver is either the tight end or the fullback and is always the opposite of the Mike-Hot receiver since the routes of the two receivers are designed to be compatible in this way. The read of the Blood linebacker becomes part of a one-two or Mike-Blood combination read. Actually, the Blood read is a second read which follows that of the Mike linebacker and is contingent upon the movements of both Mike and Blood. If the quarterback reads "Mike to hook," he automatically checks Blood's movement. The Blood read is now similar to the Mike read. If Blood blitzes or vacates the flat zone by covering another short zone instead, the Blood-Hot receiver calls out "Hot" to the quarterback and looks for a quick dump pass to be thrown to him as he bends into the open short flat zone area. (Sometimes the tight end's ability to read the movement of the Blood linebacker is impossible due to the Blood linebacker's alignment. In this case, the read is entirely the quarterback's.) If the quarterback reads the movement of the Blood linebacker as "blitz" or "vacate," he checks to see if the Blood-Hot receiver is open for a dump pass. If the Blood read dictates "dump" from an open Blood-Hot receiver, the rest of the pattern is canceled for the short dump pass. See Diagram 4-21.

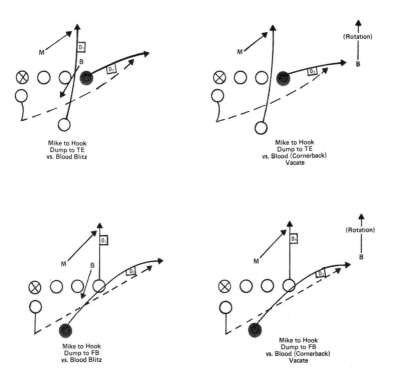

Diagram 4-21
Blood-Hot Dump Reads

If the quarterback reads "Blood blitz" or "vacate" but also reads "color" on the Blood-Hot receiver, the dump pass is canceled and the normal pass pattern is continued, as in Diagram 4-22.

If the Blood linebacker drops to his short flat zone, the Blood-Hot receiver continues on his designated route and the quarterback takes his full eight-step drop to complete his normal pass pattern reads.

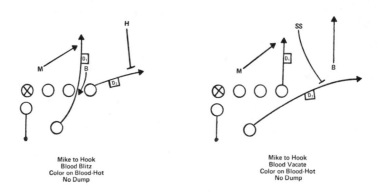

Mike to Hook
Blood Blitz
Color on Blood-Hot
No Dump

Mike to Hook
Blood Vacate
Color on Blood-Hot
No Dump

Diagram 4-22
Blood Reads—No Dump

  The double dump read is also used to check a Mike blitz or to vacate with Blood coverage the short hook zone normally covered by Mike. If the quarterback reads "Mike blitz" or "vacate" but sees the Mike-Hot receiver covered (color), he automatically checks the Blood-Hot receiver to see if he is open for a dump pass. If the Blood linebacker is covering the Mike-Hot receiver, a dump pass to the Blood-Hot receiver is dictated since the Blood-Hot receiver is open in the short flat zone. The only exception to this Blood-Hot dump pass is when the quarterback reads "color" on the Blood-Hot receiver from a rotated or inverted deep back coverage. In that case, a "color" read cancels the dump pass and continues the normal pass pattern. See Diagram 4-23.

  There is one variation of the Mike-Blood read that occurs in the Flank-Out pattern. In this pattern (discussed fully in the next chapter), the tight end, or fullback, has initial dump responsibility on his alley cut in an effort to occupy the Blood linebacker. This is done so the Blood linebacker cannot drop into the flat area under the possible hook-up cut of the flanker off of his flag cut. The same is true in the occupation of the cornerback versus a four-deep coverage: pressuring the cornerback to cover the dump threat hinders his coverage of the short flat zone underneath the flanker's flag cut. Such a hindrance helps enlarge the open area for the flanker, an area that is especially helpful versus any type of four-deep zone rotation where the flanker is forced to bend his flag cut off under the outside deep third coverage.

  The tight end, or fullback, executes his alley cut by taking off laterally to get width halfway between his original position and the

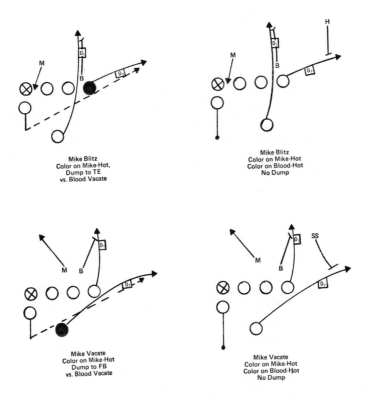

Diagram 4-23
Color Reads On Blood-Hot Receiver

flanker. Such a cut insures that the alley cut and the fly cut of the Mike-Hot receiver do not come so close together that they can be covered by one defender. See Diagram 4-24.

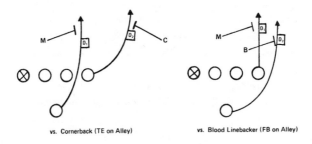

Diagram 4-24
Mike-Blood Dump Routes on Flanker-Out Pattern

In the Flanker-Out pattern, the execution of the Mike-Hot read is not changed; however, once the read is switched to the Blood linebacker or cornerback, it becomes slightly different. If the Blood linebacker or cornerback blitzes or takes a strong flat drop, the tight end bends into the most open short hook zone area and calls "Hot" to the quarterback. Once he reads "blitz" or "strong flat drop," the quarterback dumps the ball to the tight end as long as he does not see "color." The strong flat drop of the Blood linebacker, or cornerback, is actually treated as a vacate. If the Blood linebacker, or cornerback, cuts his flat drop short to cover the alley cut of the tight end, the quarterback takes his normal eight-step drop and all receivers continue their normal routes. See Diagrams 4-25 and 4-26.

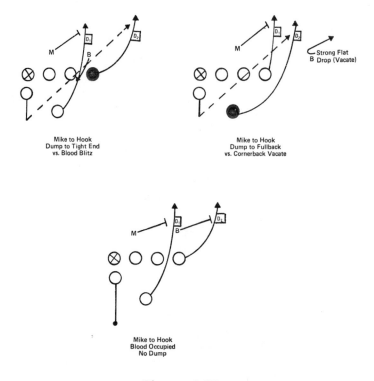

Diagram 4-25
Blood-Hot Read in Flank-Out Pattern

Diagram 4-26 shows how a fast drop by the Mike linebacker to cover the tight end's alley-fly cut and dump threat can cause the quarterback to read coverage of both dumps by one defender. If the Mike is dropping off

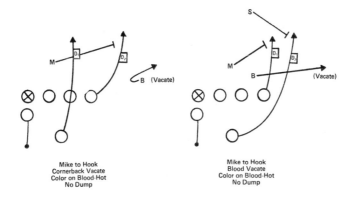

Mike to Hook
Cornerback Vacate
Color on Blood-Hot
No Dump

Mike to Hook
Blood Vacate
Color on Blood-Hot
No Dump

Diagram 4-26
Color Reads on Blood-Hot Receiver on Flank-Out Pattern

quickly, he can show initial coverage of the Mike-Hot receiver. At the same time, his quick drop can cause the quarterback to read "color" underneath the second dump read to the tight end. In this case, the quarterback simply forgets the dump and takes his normal eight-step drop to make his normal reads for the Flank-Out pattern.

If the Blood linebacker or cornerback blitzes or takes a strong flat drop and "color" occurs, the quarterback again forgets the dump and takes an eight-step drop to make his normal reads for the Flank-Out pattern. This is also shown in Diagram 4-26.

In the Split End patterns there is also a second read, but not on the Blood linebacker; instead, it is on the "Hero," or walk-away, linebacker in a three-deep secondary. Versus a four-deep secondary, he is the cornerback against an umbrella coverage and the weak safety if he is inverted with the cornerback playing a deep defensive halfback position. See Diagram 4-27.

In the Split End series, the Mike read is the same with the exception that only the tight end is the Mike-Hot receiver. This series calls for a Blue set in which the fullback is stacked behind the quarterback and involved in a pass route to the left. Thus, the quarterback is involved only in the Mike read to the tight end (right) side. If Mike blitzes or vacates there is a dump to the tight end on a Mike-Hot dump pass. There is no Blood read, no matter what the situation. If "color" occurs on the tight end during a Mike blitz or vacate, the quarterback just cancels his dump read to the tight end and looks to the "Hero" since there is no Blood-Hot receiver.

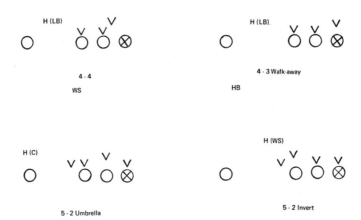

Diagram 4-27
The "Hero" Read of Various Defenses

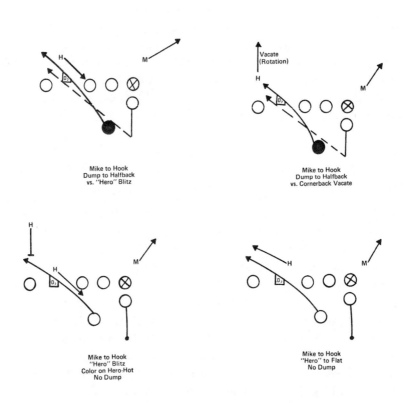

Diagram 4-28
Hero-Hot Dump Reads on Split-In Pattern

Once the quarterback reads "Mike to Hook" or "color" on the tight end as the Mike-Hot receiver, the second read is made on the walk-away linebacker, weak safety or cornerback depending on the secondary. On the Split-In pattern, the read is a simple one: if the "Hero" blitzes or vacates the short flat zone, the ball is dumped to the halfback on a shute route; if the "Hero" blitzes or vacates but "color" occurs on the halfback, the dump pass is canceled; and if the "Hero" takes a short flat zone drop, there is no dump and the normal pattern is carried out. See Diagram 4-28.

In both the Blood-Hot and Hero-Hot responsibilities, the shuting (shute cut) tight end and the left halfback cannot read any Blood or Hero blitzes or vacates and therefore, cannot help the quarterback by making a "Hot" call. They are on a 30°-angle cut with their backs turned to the defense. This is the same for the tight end and fullback on their shute cuts in the Flank-In pattern. In their initial few steps of the shute cut, they must check the quarterback to see if a dump pass is being thrown to them. The Hero read on the Split-Out pattern is actually a mirrored read of the Flank-Out read of the Blood linebacker or cornerback. On the Split-Out pattern, however, it is the halfback who runs the alley cut in an attempt to occupy the walk-away linebacker, weak safety or cornerback. If the Hero read blitzes or vacates by taking a strong flat drop, the quarterback checks the halfback for a possible Hero-Hot dump pass. If "color" occurs on the halfback, the quarterback simply forgets the dump pass and setup at eight steps to make his normal reads. See Diagram 4-29.

SEAM THEORY AND FLOATING CUT SYSTEM

Two important concepts in the drop-back series are the seam theory and the floating cut system. With the exception of the Tight-Delay pattern and the Max patterns, all patterns in the drop-back series use the seam theory. In this theory, the design of each pass pattern places a receiver in all five short passing zones, shown in Diagram 4-30, or at least in successive (usually four) short passing zones, to exploit any uncovered short zone.

Few defenses allow an uncovered deep passing zone versus a strong passing team; thus, the three-deep zones are covered almost at all times to prevent the quick score on a "bomb." The most a defense can cover short, therefore, is four of the five short passing zones unless it uses only a three-man line. For example, maximum pass coverage from a 4-4 defense, using a straight 3-deep, four short zone leaves the middle short pass zone open, as shown in Diagram 4-31.

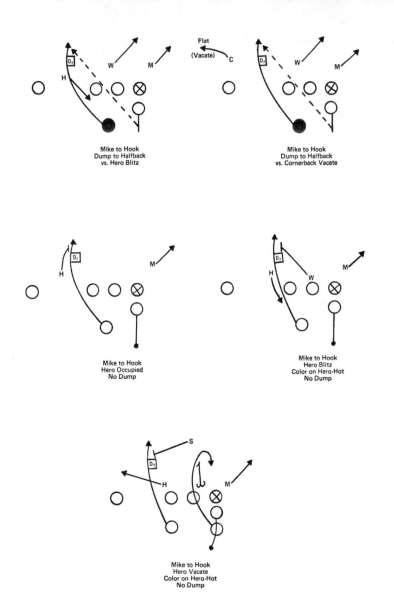

Diagram 4-29
Hero-Hot Dump Reads on Split-Out Pattern

Flat	Hook	Middle	Hook	Flat

Diagram 4-30
The Five Short Passing Zones

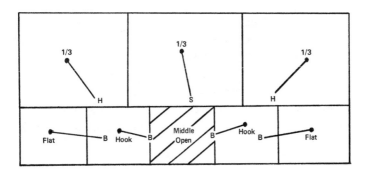

Diagram 4-31
4-4 3-Deep, 4 Short Zone Coverage
Leaving The Middle Short Passing Zone Open

The purpose of pass patterns is both to put a receiver into or through all five short passing zones and simultaneously to place receivers in between the pass defenders, thereby positioning them in the open seams and enabling the offense to exploit any open short passing zone. Receivers are placed in all five short passing zones, or successive short passing zones, by using two sideline routes (the flat zones), two hashmark routes (the hook zones) and one midfield route (the middle zone). When a receiver concentrates on fulfilling his designated route, he not only helps to exploit any open passing zone, but he also insures that no two receivers are in the same passing zone. Thus, no one pass defender can cover two or more receivers.

The ability of a receiver to penetrate the open seam, and thus be open to receive a pass, is aided by the floating cut system. Illustrated in Diagram 4-32, the system is that all receivers have the freedom to break into the most open area of their designated passing zone in an effort to get

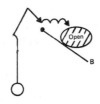

Diagram 4-32
Example of Floating Cut System (Post Hook-Up Cut Used)

open to receive a pass. If a receiver is on a post hook-up cut (explained in the next section of this chapter) that places him into the short hook zone and he finds a linebacker directly in front of him, he has the freedom to slide across the zone, or "float," and get into an open area of the zone.

Diagram 4-33 shows how the Flank-In pattern puts a receiver in or through five short passing zones to exploit the open zone or zones. The pattern puts receivers in the seams of the pass defense by using the seam theory and floating cuts to get receivers into the most open areas of the zones.

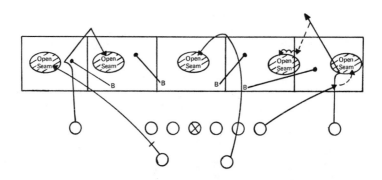

Diagram 4-33
Example of Seam Theory & Floating Cut System
(Flank-In Pattern Used for Example)

HOOK-UP OPTION

Where the dump system and forcing of coverage-and-a-half helps to control blitzing and prevent more than seven-man fronts, the hook-up and shute-up options help to control man-to-man and zone pass coverages. The philosophy is simple: throw under the deep zone and bust deep on man-to-man coverages.

In the Flanker and Split-End patterns, the call side (Flanker or Split End as called in the huddle by the play call) has hook-up options. In Diagram 4-34, the hook-up option is shown by the broken line symbol. On designated post, flag, fly and deep cuts, the receiver has the option of hooking up if he reads zone coverage or busting deep if he reads man-to-man coverage. Only receivers read the deep backs; the quarterback reads the linebackers so he can check blitzing. Once he has read the designated linebackers, he gets no further deep back read assignments since this is too much responsibility for a high school quarterback. Limit-

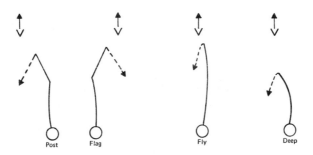

Diagram 4-34
Hook-Up on Hook-Up Option Vs. Zone Read

ing the quarterback reads greatly aids the effectiveness of the offense through further simplification. Once the quarterback finishes his dump reads, he simply sets up and reads his receivers to find the receiver left open. The receiver reads the deep back movement on his first step off the line of scrimmage. If his key drops straight back, he reads "zone," drives as deep as he can in his cut to get the zone to deepen and cuts his post, flag, fly or deep pattern short by hooking up underneath the zone coverage.

To signal the comeback or hook-up cutoff of the post, flag or fly cut, the optioning receiver throws his far (outside) arm up into the air as he plants his outside foot for the comeback cut. Throwing the arm up helps to bring the body under control since the body weight shifts toward the back portion of the ball of the foot enabling a sharper comeback cut. More importantly, the arm signal tells the quarterback to "Throw the ball, I'm coming back *now*!" The quarterback is signaled to drill the ball at the receiver's chest on a comeback (hook-up) cut off of his post, flag or fly pattern. The arm signal is given on the fourth step after the cut following the veer maneuver on the post and flag cuts. Off the fly cut, the arm signal is given at an approximate depth of sixteen yards. It is not given on the deep pattern since the hook-up cut is not a sharp cut, but more of a rounded-out cut into the short middle zone area. In addition, since the fullback's or tight end's deep hook-up cut is a secondary read for the quarterback he probably never sees the arm signal anyway.

If the receiver's deep back read shows movement in any direction other than straight back, such movement is treated as man-to-man coverage. See Diagram 4-35.

Man-to-man coverage dictates busting deep on the hook-up option rather than hooking up, as in Diagram 4-36.

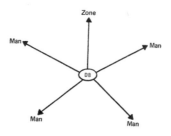

Diagram 4-35
Deep Back Read of Zone or Man-to-Man Coverage

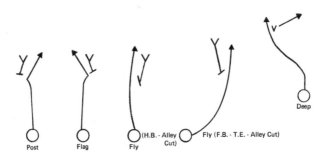

Diagram 4-36
Bust on Hook-Up Option Vs. Man-to-Man Read

Although the deep back release into another deep zone other than his own is usually part of a rotated or combination zone coverage, it is still treated as man-to-man, which dictates busting deep. A receiver busting deep and bending into the vacated seam is extremely difficult to cover by a deep back coming across field from a different deep zone. Running forward at top speed, the receiver has a great advantage on the backpedaling deep back also handicapped by his crossfield coverage responsibility. See Diagram 4-37.

On all hook-up options, there is one general rule for the receivers: when in doubt whether the coverage is zone or man-to-man, hook-up. This situation often arises on a deep back with man-to-man responsibility who tries to maintain a pad of five to six yards to prevent getting beat deep. Such a hanging deepback, who is really not showing zone or man-to-man tendencies on the first few steps the receiver takes, should be treated as zone coverage. The receiver should burst as deep as possible to

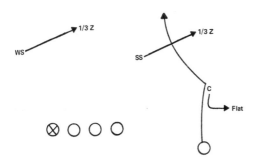

Diagram 4-37
Man-to-Man Read Vs. Rotated Zone Coverage (Post Cut
Bent Up Away From Zone Rotation of Weak Safety)

get the deep back to drop back and then hook-up. Even though the deep back may be right on top of the receiver, he has a better chance of making the reception by coming back to the ball with the receiver using his back to screen out the deep back.

The keys for the hook-up options vary with the receiver, the pattern and the defensive coverage. The main keys are the safeties (safety versus a three-deep secondary); however, such keying is discussed explicitly in the section on individual patterns in Chapter 5.

SHUTE-UP OPTION

As previously mentioned, the shute-up option is also used to control zone or man-to-man coverage. On designated cuts in the Flanker, Split-End and Tight End series, the tight end, fullback or halfback has the option of remaining shallow on his shute cut or busting up the sidelines deep, again trying to stay under the zone and bust deep versus a man-to-man coverage. The receiver keys the outside deep back or cornerback to his side while on his initial 30° angle shute cut. (If the receiver has dump responsibilities, he makes his shute-up read after he has checked to see whether or not the quarterback is dumping the ball to him.) If the receiver reads "zone" (the deep back or cornerback dropping deep), the shute cut is strung out and run shallow to stay underneath the zone. On all shute cuts, the receiver bends up the sideline once he gets four yards from the sidelines; however, versus zone coverage, he does not bust up the sidelines hard but continues to try to string out the cut and stay shallow underneath the deep zone coverage, as shown in Diagram 4-38.

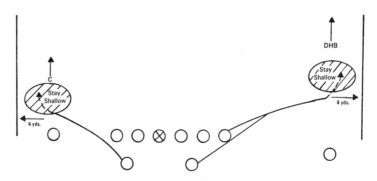

Diagram 4-38
Zone Read on Shute Cut With Receiver Remaining Shallow

If the receiver reads man-to-man coverage (the deep back or corner-back coming up tight), the shute cut is "busted" up deep up the sidelines to become a shute-up cut. See Diagram 4-39.

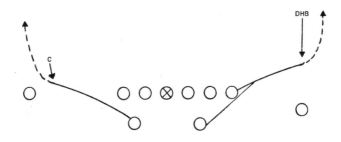

Diagram 4-39
Man-to-Man Read on Shute Cut

The same principle of busting up deep on a rotated zone coverage by treating it as a man-to-man coverage is used. If the cornerback or deep back comes up hard on a roll-up type of rotation, the shute cut receiver busts up the sidelines and switches his key to the next deep back. If the receiver can beat the rotating deep back deep, he continues to bust up deep and hugs the sidelines to stay away from the rotation. If the deep back can rotate over to the outside third and get deep position on the receiver, he throttles his speed down and hangs in between the deep coverage and the flat coverage. See Diagram 4-40.

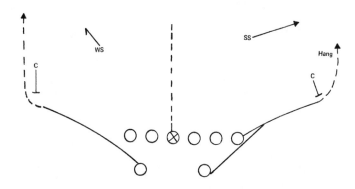

Diagram 4-40
Man-to-Man Read Vs. Rotated Zone Coverage (Bust Deep If You Can Beat Rotating Deep back, Hang in Between Deep & Flat Coverage If You Can't)

DROP-BACK PASS BLOCKING

There are two types of blocking in the drop-back passing game —marriage and maximum blocking. Maximum blocking, which provides the quarterback with the maximum amount of protection for the short passing game of the Max Pass Series, is the type of blocking for which the series is named. Rather than five receivers, as few as two and at the most four are used in the Max Series Pass patterns; everyone else is involved in the pass blocking. The Max Series is a short passing game to the wide receivers in which the quarterback must be able to throw the ball. This is the reason for the maximum amount of protection. See Diagram 4-41.

Since the quarterback is throwing off of a two-, four- or six-step drop, the line blocking is aggressive, fire-out blocking in which the linemen aim their noses at the belt buckle of the defensive linemen and linebackers if they are blitzing or tight to the line of scrimmage. The object of the blocking is to prevent the defensive linemen or linebackers from knocking the quarterback's pass down, since he is throwing so close to the line of scrimmage. The linemen must be sure not to dive to the ground or at the ankles of the defense. Defensive linemen or blitzing linebackers can jump over such a diving lineman and knock the quarterback's pass down or pressure him to throw a poor pass.

The second type of pass blocking in the Drop-Back Passing Series is marriage pass blocking. Used in the Split Series, Flank Series and Tight End Series, this block assigns a lineman or back to every defensive lineman and linebacker in the defensive front. As previously mentioned,

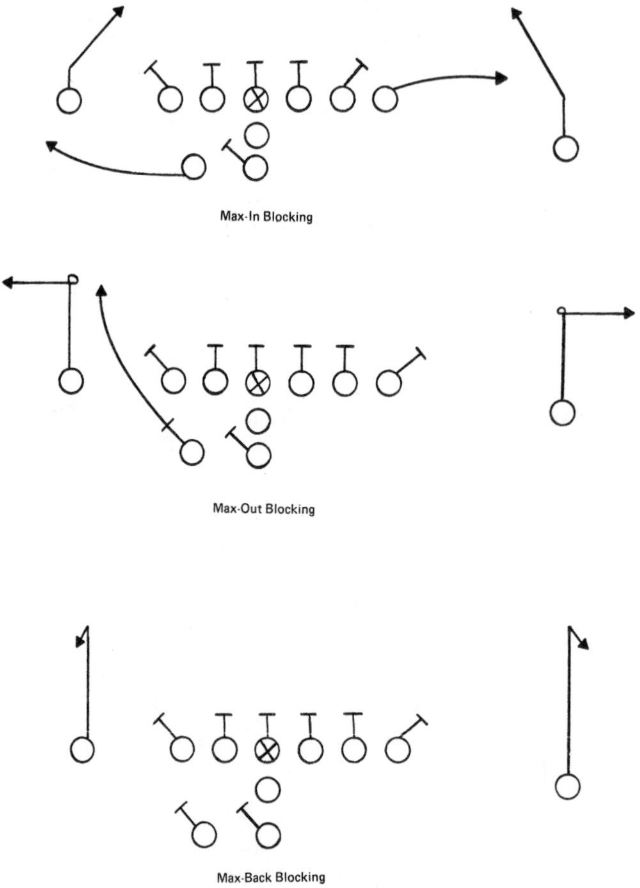

Max-In Blocking

Max-Out Blocking

Max-Back Blocking

Diagram 4-41
Maximum Pass Blocking

the marriage pass blocking can handle up to seven pass rushers. This is why it is so vital that the Max Series forces walk-away or cornerback coverage to prevent the defense from utilizing an eight-man front and rush. Marriage pass blocking is preferred over the more common cup pass blocking because it is more precise; there are no excuses or confusion as to whose man sacked the quarterback. Cup pass blocking often allows a player the excuse to sidestep responsibility for an unblocked pass rusher by claiming another man was more dangerous: "I had to help Bill out," or "I thought he was Jim's responsibility." Cup blocking also is difficult when the defensive rush overloads one side or the other.

The marriage assignments for the blockers are as follows:

1. Covered linemen: If you are covered on the line of scrimmage, you are married to that man and pass block him wherever he goes. (This does not pertain to the tight end.)
2. Uncovered center: Check for blitzing Mike linebacker. If he blitzes, you are married to him. If he drops off into pass coverage, release to tight end side and help where needed.
3. Uncovered guard (Tight end side): Check for blitzing linebacker you are assigned to. If he blitzes, you are married to him. If he drops off into pass coverage, release outside to your side and help where needed.
4. Uncovered guard (Weak side): Release immediately to outside side and block the first defensive lineman beyond your defensive tackle's man. You probably will have to pick up the defensive end. (If the linebacker in front of you blitzes, he is the responsibility of the halfback, not you.)
5. Uncovered tackle: Lane block to outside. You are married to the first defensive lineman to your outside (probably the defensive end). Maintain an inside-out position and wall him off to the sidelines.
6. Back: If you are assigned a block-shute, block-hook or block-fly route, check your assigned linebacker. If he blitzes, you are married to him. If he drops off into pass coverage, continue into your assigned pass cut.

An uncovered lineman is an offensive lineman not covered by a defensive lineman; an offensive lineman covered by a linebacker is still considered uncovered, even though he may have marriage pass blocking responsibilities with that linebacker. Lane blocking by the tackle actually marries the tackle to the first down defensive lineman to his outside. See Diagram 4-42.

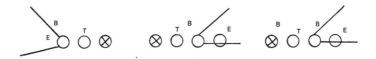

Diagram 4-42
Examples of Tackle's Lane Block Assignments

Diagrams 4-43 and 4-44 show examples of the marriage pass blocking scheme versus an odd and even defense. The Flank-In pattern is used for the examples.

Everyone in the defense is covered or married with the exception of the Blood linebacker, covered by the design of the dump system. If he

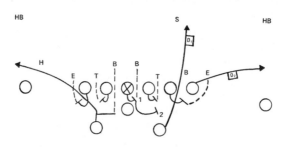

Diagram 4-43
Marriage Pass Blocking Vs. an Even Defense

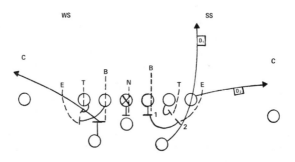

Diagram 4-44
Marriage Pass Blocking Vs. an Odd Defense

were to blitz, the quarterback could check the blitz by dumping the ball either to the fullback or the tight end, depending on the movement of the Mike linebacker and the rest of the pass coverage.

Diagram 4-44 shows the release of the left guard immediately to pick up the defensive end. As discussed in the blocking assignments, if the Willie (weakside) linebacker blitzes, the halfback, not the guard, must block him.

In all block-shute, block-hook and block-fly assignments, either the halfback or the fullback is assigned to the Willie linebacker. If the Willie linebacker blitzes, the assigned back picks him up. If Willie drops off into pass coverage, the back goes into his assigned cut. There is one addition to this general rule: the back actually has the assignment of blocking the Willie linebacker first and the Hero linebacker second (walk-away linebacker, cornerback or weak safety) if they blitz. Since his alignment, controlled by the Max passing series, usually puts him in some type of walk-away coverage, a Hero rarely ever blitzes. A blitz from that far out usually is ineffective and thus rarely attempted; however, the quarterback should not be blindsided from the rear, even if he does get the pass off. The biggest fear is that just before the snap of the ball, the cornerback, walk-away linebacker or weak safety may cheat in tight to a position where his blitz could be dangerous.

The back assigned the block on the Willie linebacker, therefore, also must be aware of a possible Hero Blitz. After he reads the Willie linebacker, the back must check the Hero linebacker. On his shute cut, this is no problem since the shute cut and the Hero's blitz are in direct line. The same is true when the back is on alley cut: the only need for an extensive check on the Hero linebacker is for the fullback on his block-hook assignment. After he reads the Willie linebacker, the fullback has to make a deliberate check of the Hero linebacker before he releases on his hook cut.

An aid in alerting the blocking back to a possible blitz from the Hero linebacker is by noticing the Hero's cheated up alignment. The halfback, aligned slightly inside the tackle, is in an excellent position to view any such cheated alignment or "sneaking up." Even if the fullback is the back with the blocking assignment in the Blue set, the halfback easily can tip off the blitz possibility by simply calling out "Check Hero, Check Hero!" When the halfback makes such a call to the fullback, it is important for the fullback to acknowledge the warning by answering, "Check," insuring that he has received the warning and is aware of the blitz threat.

5

Attacking the Secondary:
The Drop-Back Pass Series

Chapter 5 demonstrates how receiver cuts, the dump system, the seam theory and receiver options on their cuts enables the passing game to control man-to-man and zone coverages, spread the defense and control blitzing.

The Drop-Back Passing Series is actually composed of four parts, or mini-series: the Max Series, Flanker Series, Split End and Tight End Series. Utilizing the name of the prime receiver, or the term ''Max'' signifying maximum blocking aids the offensive players in grouping the related concepts that comprise the entire Drop-Back Passing Series. The eleven pass patterns of the series are sophisticated in operation, which leads to their effectiveness and explosiveness. However, basic and repetitive skills and maneuvers help the individual players to limit the skills they must learn and perfect. The only complicated part of learning and perfecting the Drop-Back Passing Series is coordinating all the individual assignments in the pass patterns, a task made easier by the fact that there are only eleven pass patterns. Three of the eleven, the Max Series, are so simple that they present no problem at all. Therefore, it reduces to a matter of continual practice in developing the coordination of eleven pass patterns, three simple ones and eight relatively easy.

THE MAX SERIES

The initial mini-series in the Drop-Back Passing Series is the Max Series. Termed ''Max'' to signify the maximum blocking, the series is a

62

short passing game series used to spread the defense or to get vital short yardage needed on a short yardage down.

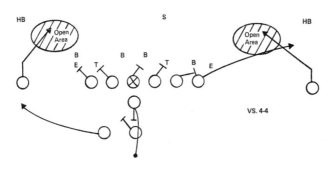

Diagram 5-1
"Blue, Max-In"

Line:	Aggressive Max fire-out blocking.
Split End:	Max-In cut into most open area. Look for ball immediately.
Tight End:	Run a fast flat shoot cut. Don't interfere with the delivery of the ball to the flanker.
Flanker:	Max-In cut into the most open area. Look for ball immediately.
Halfback:	Flare cut to sideline.
Fullback:	Aggressively block Willie if he blitzes or any seepage that occurs.
Quarterback:	By reading the defensive alignment before the ball is snapped, you must determine which wide receiver you are passing to. The pass is made on a two-step drop which opens to the receiver you are throwing to. If "color" appears on the wide receiver, throw to halfback (split end side), tight end (flanker side) or out of bounds if the secondary receivers are covered.

The actual philosophy of the Max-In pass pattern is discussed in Chapter 1. To reiterate, a major purpose of the Max-In pattern is to exploit the open short hook zone left open by a defensive alignment. Thus, as Diagram 5-1 shows, a 4-4 gap eight defense utilizing an eight-man front cuts off the run game and hinders the offense's ability to drop back pass since there is an eight-on-seven blocking mismatch for either a run or pass. The Max-In pattern repeatedly exploits what is revealed and eventually forces the defense out of an eight-man front by utilizing some sort of walk-away or cornerback coverage.

The Max-In is also used for needed short yardage; an example of this is versus a Split-6, 4-4 defense as shown in Diagram 5-1. Usually walk-away coverage-and-a-half can be forced to the split end side, but such

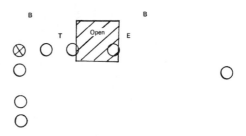

Diagram 5-2
Blocking Mismatch Vs. 4-4 Walk-away Linebacker to Flanker Side

coverage to the flanker side is rarely seen because of a blocking mismatch off-tackle by the tight end, if the Blood linebacker is placed in a walk-away position. See Diagram 5-2.

As mentioned in Chapter 1, most teams feel they can cover the Max-In cut of the flanker with both the flat release of the Blood linebacker and the help given by the safety, usually cheated over to the tight end side against a pro set. By throwing only to the Max-In cut by the flanker at vital opportunities, the Blood linebacker is often "lulled to sleep" thinking a quick flat coverage is not important. Thus, the completed Max-In cut pass is accomplished easily with an excellent chance for first-down yardage in a short yardage situation.

It is important that the wide receivers break their cuts into the most open vacated areas to gain as much yardage as possible; however, assuring a short gain by catching the ball safely in an open zone is of greatest concern.

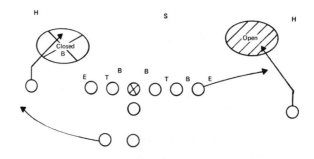

Diagram 5-3
Max-In Cut Closed Off to Split End Side,
Open to Flanker Side

The quarterback must determine which side he will throw to before the snap. Thus, if there is a walk-away linebacker to the split end side versus a 4-4 defense, the quarterback should automatically go to the flanker side.

To whatever side the quarterback predetermines his throw, he does not have the time off of a two-step drop to return to the other side. Thus, if "color" appears on the prime receiver (flanker or split end), the quarterback scans to the tight end (flanker side) or the halfback (split end side) for a safety valve receiver. If they are covered, the quarterback must throw the ball out of bounds immediately. See Diagram 5-3.

The Blue set is the best set to run the Max-In pattern from since the halfback can move into his flare cut quickly and still have good inside blocking help to the split end side by the fullback. Also, the Blue set balances the formation and often forces the safety to play "centerfield" more and prevents his overloading to the tight end side.

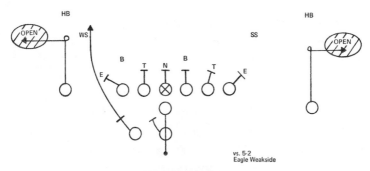

Diagram 5-4
"Blue, Max-Out"

Line:	Aggressive Max fire-out blocking.
Split End:	Max-Out cut. Look for ball as soon as outside turn is made.
Tight End:	Aggressive Max fire-out block on defensive end.
Flanker:	Max-Out cut. Look for ball as soon as outside turn is made.
Halfback:	Run block-alley fly cut. If the weak safety blitzes, block him. If he drops into pass coverage, occupy him.
Fullback:	Aggressively block Willie if he blitzes or any seepage that occurs.
Quarterback:	By reading the defensive alignment before the ball is snapped, you must determine which wide receiver you are going to pass to. The pass is made off of a four-step drop which opens to the receiver you are throwing to. If "color" appears on the wide receiver, "pump" him up, drop back two more steps and throw the deep pass to him or out of bounds if "color" remains.

The Max-Out pattern, like the Max-In pattern, allows control of the defensive alignment by forcing walk-away or cornerback coverage to cut down on the eight-man front possibility. It, too, offers an excellent short yardage pass play which focuses on exploiting the open short flat zone, as shown in Diagram 5-4. The 5-2, double invert defense cuts off the Max-In pattern, but the Max-Out pattern is left wide open. (The 5-2, double invert defense is used here for example only since it does not necessitate Max passing action because the defense is in a seven-man front. Any of the other Drop-Back Passing Series are effective against a 5-2, double invert defense.)

Another example of the Max-Out pattern occurs when trying to cut down an eight-man front in a 4-4 defense when the defense has inverted its halfbacks to cut off the Max-In pattern.

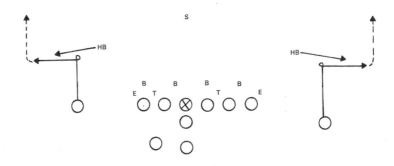

Diagram 5-5
Max-Out Pattern to Force Walk-away Coverage
Vs. a 4-4, Double Invert Alignment

As Diagram 5-5 shows, the inverted halfbacks cut off the offensive Max-In pattern; but the Max-Out pattern is left wide open. In addition, if the halfbacks come up trying to cut the Max-Out pass off, the quarterback simply can pump the wide receiver deep for the ''homerun'' pass. Few teams risk the possibility of losing deep coverage and would rather break down the eight-man front by utilizing walk-away coverage. Such pump-up action is actually for both wide receivers so that the quarterback has two possible receivers to throw to on deep bust-up cuts. This is very important versus a three-deep secondary where the middle safety may try to get deep to one side to cover a pump-up cut. In this case, however, he can only cover one of the two receivers.

Timing is essential in the Max-Out pattern. The wide receivers must look for the ball immediately upon turning on their reverse pivot to the outside; they must expect the ball to be thrown and in the air as they turn. The wide receiver should expect to catch the ball a yard or so in front of his turn as he makes his first stride to the sideline.

The quarterback again must predetermine the side he throws to. If there is an invert coverage versus a four-deep secondary to one side and normal cornerback coverage to the other, the pass is made to the invert side. See Diagram 5-6.

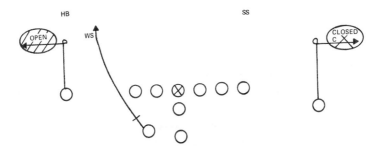

Diagram 5-6
Max-Out Cut Closed Off to Flanker Side,
Open to Split End Side

The quarterback does not have a safety valve receiver. If the wide receiver's Max-Out cut is jumped (Diagram 5-5) and he sees "color," the quarterback "pumps" the receiver deep, drops back two more steps and throws a deep leading pass over the wide receiver's shoulder. If the quarterback pumps the wide receiver deep and he's still covered (sees "color"), the quarterback simply throws the ball over the wide receiver's head, out of bounds.

Just as in the Max-In pattern, the Blue set is the most effective set from which to run the Max-Out pattern. With the tight end staying in to give extra protection to the quarterback's four-step drop, the fullback's blocking to the left gives equal blocking to each side, as shown in Diagram 5-7.

The Max-Back pass pattern is an excellent first-down play when medium yardage is needed. It is also effective versus a loose secondary playing deep against the wide receivers, who simply burst off the line of scrimmage as hard and as fast as possible to force as much depth as they can in the secondary. At fourteen yards they come back to the outside

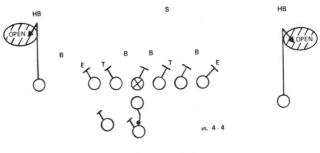

Diagram 5-7
"Blue, Max-Back"

Line:	Aggressive Max fire-out blocking.
Split End:	Run fourteen yards to twelve yards Max-Back cut. Look for low, hard driving pass to your outside.
Tight End:	Aggressive Max fire-out blocking on defensive end.
Flanker:	Run fourteen yards to twelve yards Max-Back cut. Look for low, hard driving pass to your outside.
Halfback:	Aggressively block Hero if he blitzes or any seepage that occurs to the split end side.
Fullback:	Aggressively block Willie if he blitzes or any seepage that occurs.
Quarterback:	By reading the defensive alignment before the ball is snapped, you must determine which wide receiver you are going to pass to. The pass is made off of a six-step drop which opens to the receiver you are throwing to. If "color" appears on the wide receiver, "pump" him up, drop back two more steps and throw the deep pass to him or out of bounds if "color" remains.

making a 135° angle cut. Since the quarterback must throw a low hard driving pass, the receiver must look for the ball immediately. The purpose of the play is to gain eleven to twelve yards. The receiver must not try to catch the ball and cut upfield; he will only lose yardage in the process since his hard backwards cut makes it difficult to cut upfield. Instead, receiver should catch the low, hard driving pass which may bring him to his knees ending the play. As previously mentioned, the purpose of this play is to get the first-down yardage necessary, nothing else, but the receiver must be sure to get deep enough to gain the necessary yardage: a twelve-yard gain is no good if thirteen yards were needed.

The quarterback must be aware of the yardage required, and he must realize the receiver has to break deeper if more than eleven or twelve yards are needed. The quarterback must also put plenty of "zip" on the ball in throwing the low, hard driving pass; such a pass is almost impossible to intercept.

If "color" appears on the wide receiver, the quarterback simply pumps him deep, drops back two more steps and throws the deep lead pass over his head. If on the pump-up "color" still appears, throw the ball over his head out of bounds. The Blue set, as in the other Max patterns, is again used; the tight end also stays in to give added protection.

The pump-up action by the quarterback can be utilized on any of the Max patterns. Once the receivers see the arm pump fake of the quarterback, they simply turn upfield for two steps with as great a burst of speed as possible, on the third step looking over their inside shoulders for the ball. The dump pass system is not used in the Max series: the maximum pass blocking, plus the quick development of the pass plays, cuts down on the defense's ability to use stunts to stop the quarterback's pass.

The Max patterns are the first three plays in the automatic, or audible series. The quarterback automatically checks off any other play called if the defense is using more than a seven-man front and changes the call to a Max pattern, preferably the Max-In or Max-Out. The quarterback must be aware of this in the beginning of the game before the defense is forced out of more than a seven-man front alignment. Scouting reports usually tell what strategy the defense will use; for this reason, a Max pattern can be called from the huddle or automatic to it from an audible call.

It is important to realize that this offense takes what is given. If the defense refuses to walk-away a linebacker or to utilize cornerback coverage and leaves the short flat and short hook zone open, the offense repeatedly exploits the open zones until the defense adjusts. There is no sense in running against an eight-man front when an easy six- to eight-yard gain is certain wtih a quick Max pattern. Illustrating this defensive error, one team failed to adjust to the Max-In pattern by staying stubbornly in a tight eight-man front to stop the offensive run game. The secondary was at an eleven-yard depth. Eight consecutive Max-In passes to the offensive split let him prance into the end zone untouched after covering over eighty yards in eight consecutive Max-In receptions.

Some people criticize the short flat and short hook passes as dangerous; however, the play is not called if the defensive alignment shows a defender in position to intercept. The quarterback also does not throw the pass if "color" appears by the defense but pumps the receiver deep for a long pass or throws the ball out of bounds. Secondly, Max patterns are practiced until they become second nature; they are practiced so often and demand such execution that they are almost automatic completions when called. Quarterbacks warm up by throwing Max patterns and drill them over and over in practice to develop a high level of execution and confidence. Coordination with the receivers in such drilling is of utmost importance. The receiver must coordinate his efforts with the quarterback's release of the ball to develop a sense of timing and feel for the location of the ball off of his cutting action; such timing and coordination assures the high success of the Max patterns. Many cheap touchdowns might be expected off of a flat pass interception, but this is not the case in actual practice. In fact, it is quite rare.

THE FLANKER SERIES

The second series in the Drop-Back Passing Series is the Flanker Series. The Split End and Flanker Series are outside passing series effective against both three- and four-deep secondaries. All patterns in both series focus on a prime receiver with a hook-up option either off of a flag or post cut. Coordinated with the rest of the receivers in the patterns, the Flanker Series and Split End Series patterns isolate receivers on defenders versus man-to-man coverage and throw underneath deep zone coverage. The receiver cut options allow individual patterns to adjust to individual coverages as the plays develop.

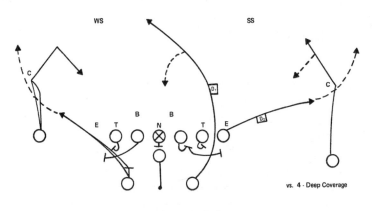

Diagram 5-8
"Red, Flank-In"

Line:	Drop-Back Passing blocking.
Flanker:	You are the prime receiver. Burst off line of scrimmage and immediately read the strong safety. If he drops straight back, read zone coverage and hook-up. If he rotates or inverts to your

	side, switch key to weak safety. If you can beat weak safety deep, treat the coverage as man-to-man and bust the post pattern deep by bending up in front of him. If you can't beat the weak safety's deep rotation, read zone coverage and hook-up. If the strong safety rotates away from you, read man-to-man coverage and bust deep bending up and away from the strong safety.
Fullback:	Read dump first; no dump, read strong safety. If safety drops straight back, read zone and hook into short middle zone. If strong safety rolls or inverts to flanker side, read man coverage and bend up deep behind weak safety's rotation and occupy him. If weak safety picks up flanker, look for deep pass. If strong safety rolls away from the flanker, also read man coverage and bend up in front of the strong safety to occupy him.
Tight End:	Run shute pattern reading dump first; no dump, read first secondary defender to outside. If cornerback or halfback drops deep, read zone coverage and hang shallow underneath zone. If defender rolls up or there is an invert, read man coverage and shute-up deep along the sidelines. If on your deep shute-up cut you see a rotated deep zone coverage placing a defender deep in front of you, throttle down and hang between the deep coverage and the flat coverage.
Split End:	Run post hook-up cut. Occupy the deep secondary defender to your side. Float into an open area as a safety valve receiver.
Halfback:	Run a block-shute cut. Pick up the Willie linebacker if he blitzes. Otherwise, run shute cut with shute-up option.
Quarterback:	Read double dump. If no dump, read post to shute to deep. If covered, scan left to hook-up and shute.

Diagram 5-8 gives the Flank-In pattern and its explanation versus a four-deep secondary. The following diagrams show how the patterns look versus various coverages with all receivers making the proper reads versus a four- and three-deep secondary.

Diagram 5-9 shows how both the flanker and the fullback hook-up versus the zone read. The tight end should actually receive the ball on the second dump read, but even if the quarterback misses the second dump read (a quick read by the quarterback may have him read "color" from the cornerback if the cornerback drops off slowly) he still returns to the tight end after his read shows "color" underneath the flanker's hook-up cut by the Mike linebacker. The tight end, reading zone coverage, hangs shallow for the flat pass either on the dump or as the quarterback continues his reads.

Diagram 5-10 shows how the flanker and the fullback bust up deep versus the zone rotation of the deep backs. As discussed in Chapter 4, any

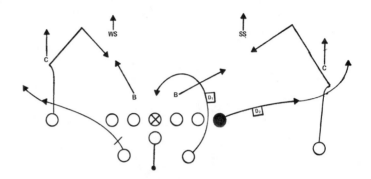

Diagram 5-9
"Flank-In" Vs. 4-Deep Zone

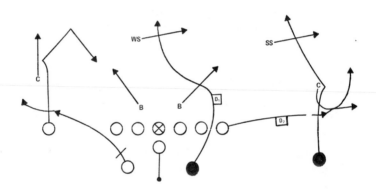

Diagram 5-10
"Flank-In" Vs. 4-Deep Rotation

read of the strong safety other than straight back is treated as man coverage. After the quarterback sees that both dumps are covered, his read of the flanker busting deep should automatically tell him man coverage. If the flanker is covered, he reads the tight end second (who in this case is covered by cornerback's flat coverage) and then the fullback's deep bust cut. The pattern actually puts the weak safety in a sweat: does he cover the flanker or the fullback? One might ask, "Why not just have the quarterback automatically go to the fullback once he sees the post bust cut covered?" The answer to this question is that he doesn't know who is covering the deep bust cut of the flanker. The flanker may have read man coverage by reading a zone rotation to the split end side, as in Diagram 5-11.

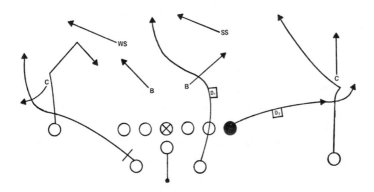

Diagram 5-11
"Flank-In" Vs. 4-Deep Rotation to Split End Side

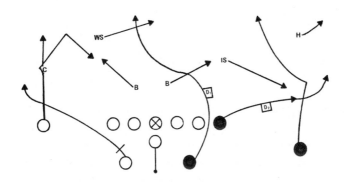

Diagram 5-12
"Flank-In" Vs. 4-Deep Invert Roll

In this case, the quarterback should read "dump" to the tight end; however, even if he misses the dump read, his read of the tight end after he sees "color" on the flanker shows him wide open in the shallow flat zone. The rotation of the secondary probably covers the flanker and fullback's deep bust cuts, but the flanker's bust cut might show him wide open deep as he bends up behind the strong safety's rotation as his cut also becomes a one-on-one isolation on the cornerback's deep drop. This is especially true if the strong safety picks up the fullback instead of the flanker, which *should* happen since it is the fullback's role to occupy the strong safety versus a split end side roll of the secondary.

Diagram 5-12 shows the "Flank-In" pattern versus a four-deep inverted roll by the safety. As soon as an inverted safety appears, the possibility of the second dump to the tight end occurs. The invert of the safety usually means he invert rolls to cover the flat, which presents an excellent one-on-one isolation on the safety; for unless he is cheated up close in his alignment and gets a good jump on the tight end, the dump to the tight end becomes a foot race up the sidelines until the halfback can come up to help. The rest of the play is run identical to the four-deep roll: the flanker and fullback again put the weak safety in a sweat over who is picked up. In all of these man-to-man read examples, the split end side cornerback is of little help to the weak safety since he is occupied by the threat of the split end busting deep, even though he is just a decoy in the Flanker patterns.

The Flank-In pattern is run identically the same versus a three-deep secondary, the only exception being that the weak safety, after reading the strong safety by the flanker and fullback, reads the offside defensive halfback. Diagrams 5-13 to 5-16 show the Flank-In pattern versus various coverages from a three-deep secondary. The offensive quarterback and receivers should think "zone" whenever a three-deep alignment occurs since few teams risk the possibility of conceding a deep zone or covering the deep secondary with only two defenders. However, some teams use such coverages to change the pace or to give extra support at the corners versus the outside run game.

In all rotations, the secondary is put into a series of "sweats." There is some type of two deep coverage with two receivers going behind the rotation if the direction of the rotation is into them. If the rotation goes away from the receivers, they again simply break behind the rotation. There also is a third deep threat from the split end since his initial cutting action fakes the post pattern to freeze the defensive halfback to his side. Even if the defensive halfback ignores the split end so the rotation to the flanker side has the offside defensive halfback and safety covering the fullback and flanker, the offense can come right back with a split end pattern to burn the strong side rotation deep.

One simple pattern can adjust to any alignment and defensive secondary movement thrown against it. Disguising coverages is of little effect, however, since the receivers do not react to alignments; instead, they react to the actual movements of the individual defenders. The total coordination may seem difficult, but it is not. Each player has only one, or possibly two, defenders to read and they are *always* the same people; he also always has the same cut with possibly one option. Since it is part of all Flank, Split and Tight patterns, the dump system becomes automatic with continual practice.

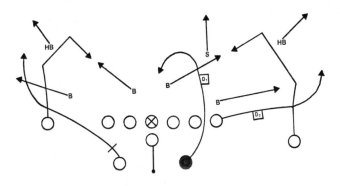

Diagram 5-13
Flank-In Pattern Vs. a 3-Deep Zone

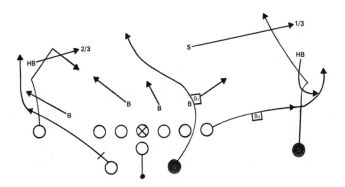

Diagram 5-14
Flank-In Pattern Vs. a 3-Deep Roll to Flanker Side

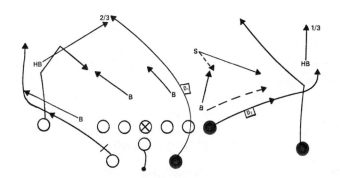

Diagram 5-15
Flank-In Pattern Vs. Safety Invert

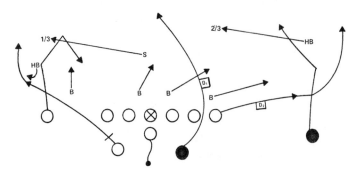

Diagram 5-16
Flank-In Pattern Vs. 3-Deep Roll to Split End Side

The quarterback is rarely expected to make more than two or three reads after he completes his dump reads. Reading two dumps, scanning to the flanker, the tight end and the fullback are enough. Scanning farther left to the split end and then to the halfback is just too much to expect. All Flank and Split series patterns have an offside receiver hooking up into the short hook zone. Once he hooks up, he becomes a safety valve receiver with the job of floating into the most open area of the hook zone and hanging in it wherever it may be. Thus, quarterbacks always know that when they are in trouble, whether it be that the receivers are covered or the pass blocking is breaking down, there is an offside receiver hanging in an open zone in the hook zone area. This is an easy thirteen- or fourteen-yard pass made slightly to the left or right of center, depending on the series. If the hook-up cut is covered, the quarterback simply throws the ball out of bounds over the shuting halfbacks head or "eats" the ball (unless the quarterback reads well enough and has time to scan to the shuting halfback).

Again, the quarterback cannot read all the way across the formation to the offside shute pattern. Offside reading is actually done from the press box with spotters quickly alerting the offense that the defense is overloading to one side or is ignoring a particular receiver. If the offside halfback is not covered in the Flank-In pattern, a Split-In pattern is called to tell the quarterback to look for the halfback's shute cut to be open.

The execution of the Flanker Series pattern and the two Split Series patterns utilizes the same theories of combating man-to-man and zone coverages, except that the patterns are different. The Flank-In pattern has been diagrammed and explained concerning individual roles of the receivers and the quarterback. Diagrams 5-9 to 5-16 showed how one pattern includes the built-in mechanisms to combat a three- or four-deep secondary and man-to-man or zone coverages. The eight diagrams explicitly show the Pro-Read Option theories in operation against all major types of coverages, and the development of such conceptual understanding now can be applied to the rest of the patterns in the Flanker and Split End Series without such extensive diagramming versus each and every coverage.

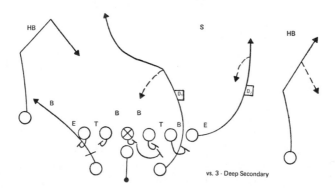

Diagram 5-17
"Red, Flank-Out"

Line:	Drop-Back Pass blocking.
Flanker:	You are the prime receiver. Burst off the line of scrimmage and immediately read the outside deep back covering you. If he drops straight back, read zone coverage and hook up. If he comes up to play you man-to-man or to cover the flat, read man coverage and bust deep on your flag pattern. Once you bust deep, switch your key to the strong safety to see if there is a rotation to your side. If there is, flatten out your flag cut more toward the sideline so it will be more difficult for his deep outside third rotation to cover you.
Tight End:	Run an alley-fly cut with dump responsibility. Your dump threat helps occupy the Blood linebacker and hinders his ability to cover the short, flat zone underneath the flanker's flattened out flag cut versus a rotated four-deep zone coverage. Occupy the strong safety. If he drops straight back, read zone coverage and hook-up. If the strong safety rotates or inverts in either direction, bust deep on fly cut if you can beat the deep back rotating towards you. If you can't, hook-up.
Fullback:	Read dump first; no dump, read strong safety. If he drops

straight back, read zone coverage and hook into short middle zone. If the strong safety rolls or inverts to the flanker side, read man coverage and bend up deep behind the weak safety's rotation (the offside halfback versus a three-deep secondary as in Diagram 5-17) and occupy him. If the weak safety picks up the tight end, look for deep pass. If the strong safety rolls away from the flanker, also read man coverage and bend up in front of the strong safety to occupy him.

Split End: Run post hook-up cut. Occupy the deep secondary defender to your side. Float into an open area as a safety valve receiver.

Halfback: Run a block-shute cut. Pick up the Willie linebacker if he blitzes. Otherwise, run a shute cut with shute-up option.

Quarterback: Read double dump; if no dump, read flag to fly to deep. If covered, scan left to hook-up and shute.

The Flank-Out pattern is an excellent isolation pattern pitting the flanker against the defensive halfback or cornerback and the tight end against the strong safety. The flanker, the prime receiver, is aided by the tight end's occupation of the strong safety; however, any type of rolls or inverts helps create a two-on-one mismatch either on the weak safety (offside defensive halfback in a three deep coverage) when the roll or invert is to the flanker side, or on the strong safety when the roll is away from the flanker. The two-on-one mismatch is created by the deep bust patterns of the tight end and the fullback plus the aid of the split end's decoy threat of busting deep on a post cut.

As in all Flanker and Split End patterns, receivers have the option of hooking up under deep zone coverages or under rotated zone coverages, if a rotated deep back can beat the receiver deep. The flanker's possible hook-up cut in the Flank-Out pattern is aided by the occupation of the outside linebacker or the cornerback by the dump pass threat to the tight end. The pressure placed on the outside linebacker or cornerback to cover that dump threat hinders their ability to drop into the flat zone quickly and get under any possible hook-up cut by the flanker or to give support under a flattened out flag cut if the coverage is a rotated zone coverage.

The Flanker Series patterns are run from the Red set to facilitate an easy release for the fullback on his deep cuts. The only change occasionally made in Flanker Patterns is simply to switch the assignments of the tight end and the fullback. Diagram 5-18 shows the Red, Flank-In pattern with a switch call.

The same switch call can be made for the Flank-Out pattern and offers a change of pace in the Flanker Series patterns. The fullback definitely is slower to get into his shute cut, but the tight end is that much

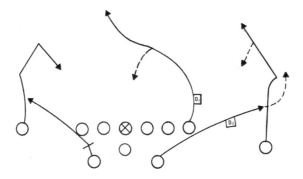

Diagram 5-18
Red, Flank-In Switch

quicker in getting into his deep cut. Again, the basic idea is to offer a change of pace since many teams try to key the tight end and fullback heavily. Such a switching of assignments can throw off such keying techniques greatly.

THE SPLIT END SERIES

The Split-In pattern, as shown in Diagram 5-19, is run much as a mirror of the Flank-In pattern. The isolation of the halfback on the weak safety is based on the same concept of isolating the strong safety on the tight end. Any type of man coverage on the shute cut by the safety is almost useless unless the safety is inverted up very tight. Also, any type of roll up or inverted coverage helps to mismatch the split end and tight end on the strong safety if the rotation is into the split end side and also mismatches the split end and tight end on the weak safety if the rotation is away from the split end. Again, the mismatch refers to the sweat that the weak or strong safety (whichever one has rotated to the deep middle zone) is placed in by deciding which deep cut to cover.

The hook cut of the fullback is often left uncovered by the short hook zone drop of the inside linebackers; it is an easy pass for the quarterback if the split end and halfback are both covered. His scan to the fullback also places his line of vision directly in line with the tight end, who may be the open receiver on his deep fly cut due to secondary rotation.

In both the Split-In and Split-Out patterns, the quarterback has a safety valve receiver in the short hook zone, just as in the Flanker Series patterns. If the coverage is three- or four-deep zone coverage, it is the fly hook-up cut of the tight end. If the coverage is man-to-man or any kind of secondary rotation, it is the post hook-up cut of the flanker underneath the fly cut of the tight end.

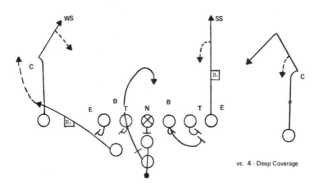

vs. 4 - Deep Coverage

Diagram 5-19
Blue, Split-In

Line:	Drop-Back Pass blocking.
Split End:	You are the prime receiver. Burst off the line of scrimmage and immediately read the weak safety (safety versus a three-deep secondary. The split end does not read the walk-away linebacker as the weak safety unless he is deep enough—seven yards or more). If the weak safety drops straight back, read zone coverage and hook up. If the strong safety rotates or inverts to your side, switch your key to the strong safety (offside halfback versus a three-deep secondary). If you can beat the strong safety deep, treat the coverage as man-to-man and bust the post pattern deep by bending up in front of him. If you can't beat the weak safety's rotation, read zone coverage and hook up. If the weak safety rolls away from you, read man-to-man coverage and bust deep, bending up and away from the weak safety.
Halfback:	Run shute cut reading dump first. No dump, read first secondary defender to your outside. If cornerback or halfback drops deep, read zone coverage and hang shallow underneath zone. If defender rolls up, or there is an invert roll to your side, read man coverage and shute-up deep along sidelines. If on your deep shute-up cut you see a rotated deep zone coverage placing a defender deep in front of you, throttle down and hang between the deep coverage and the flat coverage.
Fullback:	Run block-hook cut; if Willie linebacker blitzes, block him. If

Willie drops off into pass coverage, run hook cut into short middle zone.

Tight End: Read dump; no dump, run fly cut with hook-up option. If strong safety (safety versus three-deep) drops straight back, read zone coverage and hook-up into short hook zone area. If safety rolls or inverts to either side, bust deep on your fly cut and either occupy the safety or look for deep pass to be thrown to you.

Flanker: Burst off line of scrimmage and immediately read the strong safety (safety versus three-deep). If the strong safety drops straight back, read zone coverage and turn your post hook-up cut into a quick hook cut in the short flat zone. If the strong safety rolls or inverts in either direction, run a post hook-up cut into the short hook zone.

Quarterback: Read double dump; if no dump, read post to shute. If covered, scan right to hook to fly to hook-up.

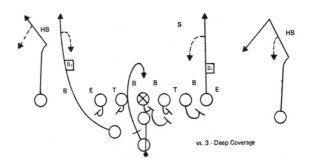

vs. 3 - Deep Coverage

Diagram 5-20
Blue, Split-Out

Line: Drop-Back Pass blocking.

Split End: You are the prime receiver. Burst off the line of scrimmage and immediately read the outside deepback covering you. If he drops straight back, read zone coverage and hook-up. If he comes up to play you man-to-man or to cover the flat, read man coverage and bust deep on your flag pattern. Once you bust deep, switch your key to the safety (weak safety versus four-deep) to see if there is a rotation to your side. If there is, flatten out your flag cut more toward the sidelines so it is more difficult for his deep outside third rotation to cover you.

Halfback: Run an alley-fly cut with dump responsibility. Occupy the safety (weak safety versus a four-deep secondary). If he drops straight back, read zone coverage and hook-up. If the safety rotates or

	inverts in either direction, you bust deep on fly cut if you can beat the deep back rotating towards you. If you can't, hook-up.
Fullback:	Run block-hook cut; if Willie linebacker blitzes, block him. If Willie drops off into pass coverage, run hook cut into short middle zone.
Tight End:	Read dump; no dump, run fly cut with hook-up option. If safety (strong safety versus four-deep) drops straight back, read zone coverage and hook up into short hook zone area. If the safety rolls or inverts to either side, read man coverage and bust deep on fly cut and either occupy the safety or look for a deep pass to be thrown to you.
Flanker:	Burst off the line of scrimmage and immediately read the safety (strong safety versus four-deep). If the safety drops straight back, read zone coverage and turn your post hook-up cut into a quick hook cut in the short flat zone. If the safety rolls or inverts in either direction, read man coverage and run a post hook-up cut into the short hook zone.
Quarterback:	Read double dump. If no dump, read flag to fly. If covered, scan hook to fly to hook-up.

The Split-Out pattern, shown in Diagram 5-20, is a close mirror of the Flank-Out pattern to the split end side. Like the Flank-Out pattern, the Split-Out pattern is an excellent isolation pattern, pitting the split end against the defensive halfback or cornerback and the halfback against the weak safety. The split end, like the flanker, is aided by the occupation of the safety, or weak safety versus a four-deep secondary by the halfback. The same two-on-one mismatch is created in the secondary versus roll or inverted rotation coverages.

There are many repetitive skills and concepts in all outside patterns of the Flanker and Split End Series. In the two patterns in each of the two series, only the flanker and tight end in the Flanker Series and the split end and halfback in the Split End Series have different assignments; the rest of the patterns remain the same. This greatly helps to lessen the amount of teaching and practice time required. In the Flanker Series, the assignments do not change for the fullback, split end and halfback. (The only exception to this is on a "switch" call in which the fullback switches assignment with the tight end.) In the Split End Series, the assignments of the fullback, tight end and flanker remain the same.

In both the Flanker and Split End Series, a safety valve receiver always hooks up into the short hook zone. In the Split End Series, it may be a different person, the tight end or the flanker; but the same idea of a receiver hooking up and floating into the most open area of the short hook zone is present.

At this point, some important concepts of Flanker and Split End patterns require emphasis: initially, the receiver must keep in mind the seam theory. All patterns put a receiver through one of the five short passing zones, or at least through four consecutive short passing zones. He must concentrate on occupying his assigned zone but does have the option to float into the most open area of that assigned zone. Even if his read tells him to bust deep in some way, he must be sure to execute his cut through his assigned short zone. Floating a cut does not mean going into or through another short passing zone. If one receiver is covered, another must be left open in another short passing zone. A common tendency of receivers is to bunch up, or get too close together. If this happens, the theory of filling open zones is nullified since one defender can cover two receivers because they are close together.

Another important idea in review commonly used in drop-back pass game teaching is the term "occupy." Whenever a receiver has an occupy assignment, he attempts to get the attention of a particular deep back so that player picks him up and plays him. The purpose of such an occupation is usually to free a prime receiver; however, if the receiver with the occupy assignment is not picked up, he must be ready to receive the pass since he probably is the open receiver.

Another important idea in the Flanker and Split End Series is the depth the wide receiver gets in his post or flag pattern, whether he hooks up or not. The purpose of the technique of "bursting off the line of scrimmage" is to cause the deep backs to increase their deep drops at a quicker pace. This action puts more pressure on the linebacker coverage since they have a greater area to cover. Also, the area left open underneath the deep zone between the deep backs and linebackers has been expanded greatly. Any hook-up action by a receiver thus gives him a wider span of area to get open in and to receive the pass. Obviously, a wide open receiver is the easiest player to receive a completed pass.

Due to this emphasis on getting as much depth as possible, it is of utmost importance to have the fastest players at the wide receiver spots. One of the most important practice emphases with wide receivers is the take-off: no wasted motion and the quickest possible release from the line of scrimmage.

The term "prime receiver" is taken literally. In both the Flanker and Split End series, the wide receiver is set up for a bust deep or hook-up option. He is the initial read after the dump reads are made, but this does not mean he is the person to whom the ball is thrown. If he's covered, another receiver must be left open. The quarterback's scan in his assigned progression helps him find out who it is.

In both the Flank-Out and Split-Out pattern, it was mentioned how the wide receiver doing the flag cut bends the cut off to the sideline if he sees a rotated deep coverage getting a defender deep in front of him. Diagram 5-21 shows this action for both the flanker and the split end.

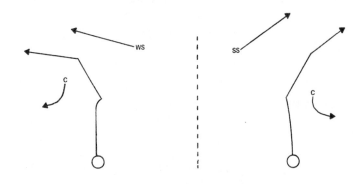

Diagram 5-21
Flattened Off Flag Cut by Wide Receiver
Vs. a Rotated Zone Coverage If
Rotated Deep Back Gets Deep Position on Him

THE TIGHT END SERIES

The last of the four mini-series in the Drop-Back Passing Series is the Tight End Series, composed of four patterns; the Tight-Delay, Tight-Across, Tight-Deep and Tight-Out. The Tight End Series is very effective versus a three-deep secondary; isolations, crossing patterns, floods and cuts running underneath zone coverages are all utilized in these series patterns.

The Tight-Delay pattern, illustrated in Diagram 5-22, is an excellent medium yardage play and also highly effective versus fast and deep drops by the linebackers. Basically, the receivers, with the exception of the flanker, clear out deep for the tight end with the assignment of occupying the two inside linebackers and the offside deep back. The occupying cuts often drag the defenders deep, opening a vacated area for the tight end to exploit. What initially is the goal of gaining six to eight yards often develops into a foot race up the split end side sideline for a long gain.

The tight end must delay for two full counts; his fake block action often forces a 4-4 type Blood linebacker to step up into the off-tackle hole. When the tight end eventually reverse pivots into his cut, the Blood linebacker is usually out of position either to react to the tight end's cut or to drop off into any type of pass coverage. In addition, the tight end's delay usually finds the linebackers disregarding him, which makes the play all the more effective.

The Tight-Delay also has the mechanism to combat any "staying-at-home" by the inside linebackers. If either the Willie or Mike linebacker quickly picks up the tight end, there is a receiver in the short hook zone to that linebacker's side. The linebacker, on whichever side he is aligned, cannot both come up tight to play the tight end and drop off to cover the short hook zone at the same time. The greatest successes of the Tight-Delay are against man-to-man coverages with the Willie linebacker assigned to the halfback's fly cut. Such coverage allows the halfback to occupy the Willie linebacker and to clear out the area for the Tight-Delay cut.

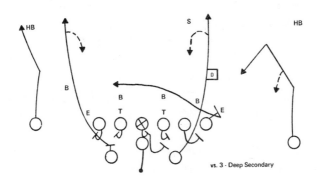

Diagram 5-22
Red, Tight-Delay

Line:	Drop-Back Pass blocking.
Split End:	Run a deep flag cut. Be more concerned with getting deep than setting up the flag cut. Try to force double coverage if you can.
Halfback:	Run a block-fly cut. If Willie linebacker blitzes, block him. If Willie drops into pass coverage, run an alley-fly cut. Occupy the Willie linebacker. If he disregards you to pick up the tight end, hook-up and look for the ball.
Fullback:	Read dump first; no dump, run fly cut and try to occupy the Mike linebacker. Drag him deep if you can. If the Mike linebacker drops off to play the tight end, hook up into the most open area of the short hook zone and look for the ball.

Flanker: Burst off the line of scrimmage and immediately read the full-
                back. If the fullback hooks up, turn your post hook-up cut into a
                quick hook cut into the short flat zone. If the fullback busts deep
                on a fly pattern, run a post hook-up cut into the short hook zone.

Tight End: Slam the defensive end for two counts with outside shoulder.
                Reverse pivot and run tight delay cut across the formation at
                approximately a 30° angle underneath the drop of the lineback-
                ers. The actual depth of the cut depends on the depth of the
                linebacker drops.

Quarterback: Read dump. If no dump, read tight across cut. If "color" ap-
                pears from the Willie linebacker area, check halfback hook-up.
                Otherwise, scan to fly to hook-up.

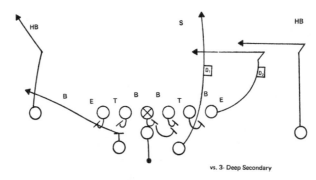

vs. 3- Deep Secondary

Diagram 5-23
Red, Tight Across

Line: Drop Back-Pass blocking.

Split End: Run a deep flag cut. Be more concerned with getting deep than
                setting up the flag cut. Try to force double coverage if you can.

Flanker: Burst off line of scrimmage; break an across cut off of a post cut
                veer release. You should come across at approximately a depth
                of eight to nine yards. Keep a distance of one full short passing
                zone between you and the tight end; you might have to throttle
                down to accomplish this. Never get too close to the tight end so
                that one defender can cover the two of you.

Tight End: Release from line of scrimmage towards the sidelines. You must
                get width as you get depth. Your alley release should put you
                halfway to the flanker. Read dump; no dump, break across field
                after a quick outside fake at approximately a depth of seven to
                eight yards.

Fullback:	Read dump; no dump, run fly cut. Try to occupy the Mike linebacker and the safety. You have no hook-up option.
Halfback:	Run block-shute pattern; if Willie blitzes, block him. If Willie drops into pass coverage, run shute pattern to try to occupy him and the walk-away linebacker, if there is one.
Quarterback:	Read double dump; if no dump, read tight across to fly to flank across.

The Tight-Across pattern, shown in Diagram 5-23, is an excellent flood pattern of the short middle and hook zones by the tight end and flanker. The flood is accomplished by a crossing pattern underneath the fullback's fly cut and takes place underneath the occupation of the safety and possibly the Mike linebacker by the fullback. Most often, the fullback draws the Mike linebacker into a deepened short hook zone coverage if the coverage is zone. If the Mike linebacker is on a man-to-man coverage assigned to the fullback, the fullback may draw him completely out of the play. For this reason, the deep fly cut of the fullback is extremely important: he *must* get deep fast to clear out the underneath area for the cuts of the tight end and flanker.

If the coverage is man-to-man with the Mike linebacker staying with the fullback and the safety picking up the tight end, a mismatch occurs deep with the isolation of the fullback's bust on the Mike linebacker deep. If the defense zone covers, the Mike linebacker is put into a "sweat" as to who to pick up—the tight end or the flanker. Many times, the Mike linebacker's preoccupation with the fullback's fly cut through his zones delays the Mike linebacker long enough to hinder his coverage of the tight end. The read to the fullback on his fly cut deep is made easily when the quarterback reads the tight end since the quarterback's line of vision enables him to see both at the same time. Thus, if the safety comes up to cover the tight end, the quarterback easily can see the fullback free deep, unless the Mike linebacker is exceptionally fast in covering the fullback.

The Tight-Deep pattern, demonstrated in Diagram 5-24, is an excellent isolation pattern in two respects: first, it floods the defensive halfback's deep zone. This is especially true when the defensive halfback comes up heavily to pressure the flanker's post and post hook-up cut whether the coverage is man-to-man or zone. Once the defensive halfback is spotted coming up on the flanker hard, a Tight-Deep is called to isolate the tight end on the safety. If the coverage is three-deep zone, the safety often may release his tight end coverage altogether once he breaks his cut for the deep outside third, figuring the defensive halfback will pick him up. Even if the coverage is man-to-man with the safety picking up the tight end, or a zone coverage with the safety deciding to stay with the tight end, the tight end's "freeze" technique on the safety usually holds him in his deep middle area long enough to make it almost impossible for the safety to cover the tight end's deep flat cut. Once such a flood and isolation are effective, the Tight-Delay pattern often becomes a big gainer since it is a deep pattern.

The second way that the Tight-Deep pattern acts as an isolation pattern is by creating a mismatch on the fullback's shute pattern. The tight

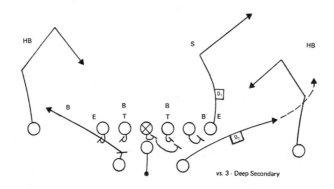

vs. 3 · Deep Secondary

Diagram 5-24
Red, Tight-Deep

Line:	Drop-Back Pass blocking.
Flanker:	Run post hook-up cut. Try to occupy the defensive halfback to your side.
Tight End:	Read dump first. No dump, burst deep on tight-deep cut. Be sure to use "freeze" technique by cutting right at the safety before making final bust deep flag cut to outside deep third.
Fullback:	Run shute cut with shute-up option. Be sure to check for dump on initial release.
Halfback:	Run block-shute cut. If Willie blitzes, block him. If Willie drops into pass coverage, run shute cut with shute-up option.
Split End:	Run post hook-up cut. Occupy the deep secondary defender to your side. Float into an open area as a safety valve receiver.
Quarterback:	Read double dump. No dump, read tight deep to hook-up to shute. If covered, scan left to hook-up to shute.

end's pressure placed on the safety eliminates any possibility of the safety covering the fullback on his shute pattern. This isolation might take place on some type of man-to-man coverage where the Blood linebacker is trying to cover the tight end. Even if the Mike linebacker is the player covering the fullback on man coverage, it is very difficult for him to cover the fullback on a dump pass. The same is true if the pass is made to the fullback on his shute cut after the quarterback reads the tight end and flanker.

The change of releases by the tight end and fullback also helps to set up the fullback's isolation on whoever is covering him. The tight end, who normally releases to the outside, now releases deep. Few teams, especially 4-4 gap eight teams, allow the tight end to release unmolested when releasing straight ahead. A "jam" technique by the Blood linebacker on the tight end side makes it very difficult to cover the fullback's shute pattern.

As previously mentioned, the Tight End Series patterns work best against three-deep secondaries. The Tight-Deep pattern is a good example of how the tight end patterns are not as effective against four-deep secondaries since the alignment of the strong safety to cover the tight end's flag cut is overshifted. Even the fullback's shute cut isolation becomes much less effective due to possible flat coverage according to the secondary coverage action.

The Tight-Out pattern, shown in Diagram 5-25, is an excellent isolation pattern which isolates the tight end on the safety by using the crossing out cut underneath the flanker's deep clear out cut. The isolation is aided by the pressure put on the safety by the fullback and tends to freeze the safety long enough to make him ineffective in covering the tight end. The tight end's out cut usually can bend up deep enough to render the Blood linebacker's coverage useless in covering the out cut.

In both the Tight-Deep and the Tight-Out patterns the quarterback again has a safety valve receiver to the offside in the form of the split end's post hook-up cut. Similarity of assignments is not as consistent as the patterns of the outside series—the Flanker and Split End Series; but the Tight End patterns give the drop-back passing game a great variety of pattern action. The Tight End Series also gives the Drop-Back Passing Series an alternate method of attacking zone and man-to-man coverages, especially effective versus three-deep secondaries.

All Tight End patterns are run from the Red set; and much like the Flanker patterns, the Red set is the best one to get the fullback into the pattern as quickly and effectively as possible.

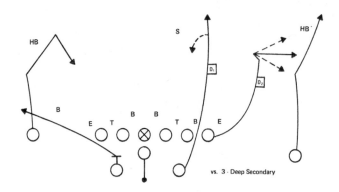

Diagram 5-25
Red, Tight-Out

Line:	Drop-Back Pass blocking.
Flanker:	Run a deep flag cut. Be more concerned with getting deep than setting up the flag cut. You must occupy the defensive halfback and clear out the area for the out cut of the tight end.
Tight End:	Release from line of scrimmage towards the sidelines. You must get width as you get depth. Your alley release should put you halfway to the flanker. Read dump. No dump, break out to sidelines at an approximate depth of seven to eight yards after a quick inside fake. Read the drop of the defensive halfback to determine depth and angle of your break and the flat coverage to find the most open area.
Fullback:	Read dump. No dump, run deep fly cut. Be sure to occupy the safety. If the safety drops straight back, hook-up. If safety rotates or inverts in either direction, bust deep on fly cut.
Halfback:	Run block-shute cut. If Willie blitzes, block him. If Willie drops into pass coverage, run shute cut with shute-up option.
Split End:	Run post hook-up cut. Occupy the deep secondary defender to your side. Float into an open area as a safety valve receiver.
Quarterback:	Read double dump. No dump, read tight out to flag. If covered, scan left to fly to hook-up to shute.

6

Developing the Pro-Read Option
Run Game

Chapter 1 explains that the purpose of the run game is to attack the weaknesses of a spread-out defensive front, whether it be inside or at the corners, by forcing coverage-and-a-half which prohibits the use of more than a seven-man front. Such a spread-out defense thus weakens the front (less players), cuts down on the defense's ability to pursue (greater distances to cover) and gives each defensive front player a greater area of responsibility. The design of the entire running game is to attack these defensive weaknesses quickly and explosively. Explosion, speed and execution are the keys to the running game, not "razzle-dazzle" or slow-developing misdirection plays. With the exception of quick hitting counter series, this strategy does not try to fool the defense; the one spread offensive formation analyzes defensive strengths and weaknesses quickly to determine where to attack and where not to. The offense takes advantage of a weakened area on the defensive front by blowing a back through the hole quickly. Not only can the offense break backs into the secondary quickly, but it also can hinder defensive pursuit greatly by the quick-hitting technique of the ball carrier.

This philosophy of the run game is a great aid to line blocking; quick-hitting plays reduce the length of time a block must be held. Although the blockers are not told this, since we want them to sustain their blocks as long as possible to prevent pursuit, an explosive take-off and proper head and body position by the linemen are usually enough to spring a ball carrier through a weakened area of the defense. Explosion and shallow depth of the running backs are keys to the success of the running game. The backs know that the quicker they hit the hole, the greater the chance it will be open. They also know the slower they hit the hole, the more difficult will be the blocking for the linemen and the less the chance of an open hole. In addition, there is a general rule for all ball carriers: if there is no open hole—make one. A good back who explodes to a hole at top speed and power can grind out a yard or two if no hole is opened. One of our greatest claims, and a fact of great pride, is that in the two years we have used the offense, we rarely ever have lost yardage on our running plays. We have been stopped for no gain, but we have rarely lost yardage. This is a great advantage to the offense. We rarely find ourselves in long yardage situations. A third down situation of six to eight yards is usually the most we are faced with. We have great confidence in our offense to pick up eight or so yards on a run or pass. Thus, we are not forced into a third and long pass situation. The defense is not able to use a prevent pass defense as we do not treat a third and six or eight situation as warranting a long pass. We continue to use defense control to pick up the needed first-down yardage.

LINE SPLITS, STANCE AND SET

Line splits, illustrated in Diagram 6-1, are also an important part of spreading the defense. The linemen should take big splits, the general rule being two feet a yard and three feet to five. However, tackles have the freedom to split up to four feet as long as the defensive alignment does not threaten penetration through the gap.

Diagram 6-1
Offensive Line Splits

If the defense tries to compensate by putting defensive linemen in the gaps and penetrating them, the linemen tighten slightly enabling us to run outside or off-tackle to take advantage of easy down blocks created. The tight end split fluctuates from a one-yard split to five feet, or a "nasty" split; it is used according to the plan of attack on the defensive front. Scouting usually helps to determine how best to utilize the tight end split versus various defensive formations, adjustments and defensive play.

Overall, the wide line splits cause the defensive front to expand and become thinner in strength.

Once the quarterback calls the play in the huddle for the first time, it is imperative that the center break from the huddle early and take his alignment and stance over the ball: he is the key for the rest of the offensive line in taking their stance and alignment. Once the huddle is broken, the linemen must sprint to the line of scrimmage, and the guard must set up quickly by aligning his toe tops of both feet on the heel of the forward foot of the center. It is imperative that both toe tops are aligned in a straight line off of the center's heels since the tackles and tight end are aligning their toe tops in a straight line off of the man next to them to the inside. Thus, a straight line with a consistent take-off is assured. Bowing the line is eliminated as long as the linemen align both of their toe tops. If they just align the inside toe top and slightly stagger the outside foot, the line bows.

Once the linemen assume their proper alignment and splits, a pre-set stance is taken: the linemen squat with their weight placed on the balls of their feet; their necks are bulled, eyes peering straight out, and feet are pointed straight ahead. The forearms rest on the thighs and fists are clenched and pointed straight ahead. This stance is an excellent one to go into a pass block on a quick count. If the defense becomes lax, the offense can even run from this stance on a quick count.

On the quarterback's set signal, the up-down set of the linemen into their stance is used. The linemen simply straighten up (stand up) and go down into their normal three-point stance; they also may stagger their feet.

BACKFIELD SET

Backfield sets and alignments are discussed in Chapter 3. It must be pointed out, however, that the backs take their alignment positions designated by the play call as soon as they break the huddle, whether it be the "I," "Red," or "Blue" set. What they do not do is take their set stance until the quarterback gives the "Set" command. Once in their alignment position they take a two-point, upright pre-set stance. Their weight must be balanced over the balls of the feet with the heels slightly off the ground; hands are placed on the thigh pads, the back is arched and the neck is bulled. This stance provides an excellent stance from which to take off on a quick count first sound starting signal. In addition, the back can use peripheral vision to see the defensive alignment and how the blocking scheme may unfold. The back must not put his hands on his knees since this causes him to become flat-footed, to have a slower start and to reduce his ability to see the defense. He also must assume this pre-set position whether or not the play is run on a quick count. If he sets his stance from the pre-stance position, he must not lapse into a sloppy pre-set stance since this is a key for the defense that he takes a proper pre-set stance for a quick count starting signal.

If the play is to be run on a "Go!" count after the "Set" signal, the backs should use the up-down technique on the "Set" signal: they simply stand straight up and take their set positions in a three-point stance.

RUN BLOCKING

There are two types of run play blocking—call and rule (or more descriptively termed assignment) blocking. Call blocking, illustrated in Diagram 6-2, is mainly used in the power series. At the hole to be run, the lineman to the outside of the hole makes a call for the two linemen involved in blocking that hole while in their upright, or pre-set stance. This is one of the reasons that the linemen's eyes must peer straight out—so they can read the defensive alignment and determine what blocking technique should be used. The call indicates how the hole is to be blocked. It is made by giving the line call plus the first name (or nickname) of the inside lineman to whom he is giving the call. An example is "Able-John," in which the Able (or straight on) blocking technique is called. The inside lineman answers by giving the same line call plus calling the name (or nickname) of the original caller, for example, "Able-Bill." All other linemen make "dummie" calls with wrong names, either "Able" or downfield blocking according to their role in the play. If necessary, linemen other than those at the live hole, can make "live" calls to block a difficult alignment. A gap stack might better be blocked with a "Baker" call (fold block) than an "Able" call. Such a live call is signified simply by using correct names or nicknames between the linemen away from the hole.

Since the "Willie" call for wedge blocking is a multiple answer call from all involved linemen, it is often used as a "dummie" call on pass plays or rule blocking plays to avoid tipping off a wedge block. A general rule for a defense that jumps into a new alignment just before the snap of the ball is automatically to "Able" block for that play and check off the previous line call. Adjustments for such defensive re-alignment are made on sideline chalkboards with the offensive linemen so that if it occurs again on the next offensive series, it can be attacked effectively.

Calls:

1. "Able":   Block the man covering you.

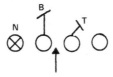

2. "Baker":   Fold block with uncovered man blocking the defensive lineman first.

If the stack is in the gap, the outside man goes first.

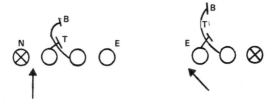

If a stack is away from the hole called, a "Baker" call still can be used with the blocker nearest the hole being run going first.

Diagram 6-2
Call Blocking

3. "Combo":   Tackle helps guard reach block the tackle in split-six look by slamming him to set up reach block before releasing to down-block the linebacker. This call can also be made between the tackle and tight end and the guard and center.

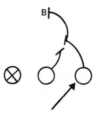

4. "Dog":   Double team block using the post-drive technique with the man closest to the hole doing the driving.

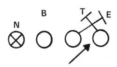

5. "Charlie":   Crossblock with outside man going first.

6. "Willie":   Wedge with the inside blocker of the hole becoming the apex of the wedge. (This is also the trouble call; when in doubt call "Willie.")

Diagram 6-2
Call Blocking (con't)

Rule blocking, as shown in Diagram 6-3, is used in the sweep and counter series and also in the power series when the defensive end must be kicked out with a back. Rule blocking simply means that the linemen and backs have certain blocking assignments rather than making a call at a hole.

1. Sweep: Down blocking with hook or kick-out block on defensive end by lead back. Off guard (with exception of 5-2 defense) pulls and blocks secondary contain.

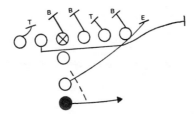

2. Counter: Down blocking with a trap on the first down lineman past the center.

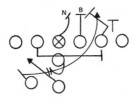

3. Kick Out: Down blocking with Ice block on defensive end.

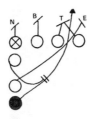

Diagram 6-3
Rule Blocking

Call blocking also can be incorporated with rule blocking by using a "Baker" call (fold block), for example, between a guard and tackle to block a split-six stack on sweep rule blocking, as shown in Diagram 6-4.

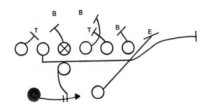

Diagram 6-4
Use of Call Block ("Baker") Within Rule Blocking

7

Utilizing the Power Series in the Pro-Read Option Attack

The power series is the most effective series due to its simplicity, balanced attack and quick-hitting explosiveness. In line with the run theories, any defensive weakness can be exploited from the off-tackle to off-tackle hole with speed and power. This series is nothing more than a first back lead block for the second back, the ball carrier through the designated hole. The quarterback fakes power pass play action, and the power plays are run from the Blue and I sets only; the Red (Split) set formation is too slow hitting for power plays. Except for kickout power plays, all powers use call blocking. The "I, Power 2" play is used as the example for this series. Its execution is explained in detail, position by position.

Diagram 7-1 shows an "Able" block by the right guard and center. When powering at the one and two hole, the offense rarely uses the "Baker" (fold block) or the "Charlie" (cross block) calls. Unless the defense is using some type of alignment requiring a "Baker" or "Charlie" block, the use of these blocks is too slow for quick-hitting power at the one and two holes.

The most effective technique in the power series is the "freeze" technique, shown in Diagram 7-2. In all power plays offensive linemen are coupled with defensive linemen in the blocking schemes; a back lead should block a linebacker if there is an extra defensive man to be blocked (Diagram 7-1). The blocking assignment is easier when the ballcarrier runs right at the linebacker (or actually any free defensive man to be blocked by a lead blocker) in an attempt to freeze the would-be tackler.

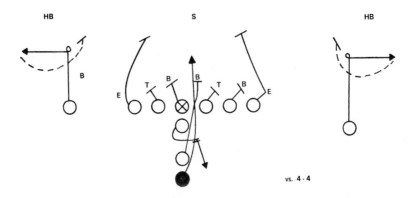

Diagram 7-1
"I, Power 2"

Live Linemen (Center and Right Guard): "Able" call shown.
Other Linemen: Able or downfield blocking.
Wide Receivers: Max-Out fake and turn in block.
Fullback: Lead block at 2 hole. Use freeze technique.
Tailback: Carry at 2 hole. Use freeze technique.
Quarterback: Reverse pivot, hand-off at 2 hole, fake power pass.

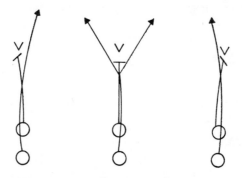

Diagram 7-2
"Freeze" Technique

When a ball carrier veers left or right toward daylight, he gives the tackler direction as to where to fill, which makes it more difficult for the blocker since he must "dig" the tackler out of the hole. By running the ball straight at the would-be tackler, the tackler (linebacker in this case) is forced to freeze his position in an effort to determine which way to angle in getting to the ball carrier, as shown in Diagram 7-2. A frozen, or sitting tackler is an easier blocking assignment for any lead blocker. This is true whether it be on a power play with a back lead or a pulling guard lead on a sweep. Once the lead blocker makes contact, the ball carrier simply breaks for daylight opposite the direction of the block being thrown or to the most open daylight—if the blocker drives his man straight back. As previously mentioned, this technique may be used in any situation, run play or pass, once a ball carrier has a lead blocker in front of him.

On all power run plays, the quarterback reverse pivots to misdirect linebacker flow; after his hand-off, he flows to the play side and sets up to fake a play action pass. The wide receivers use a Max-Out fake when a power is run up the middle to draw the deep backs up and out. This puts the deep backs out of position to flow back deep to the middle on a pursuit angle. When powers are run off-tackle or off-guard, the offense has onside wide receivers run a deep flag hook-up fake to drive the pass defenders deep cutting their ability to give support.

Diagrams 7-3 to 7-6 show the power runs at 4, 6, 1 and 3 holes. Each diagram shows the various blocking calls used against various defensive looks. Also, live call situations are shown by linemen other than at the designated hole to be run. Since defensive alignments to the split end look, where call blocking is effective, rarely occur, call blocking at the 5 hole is rarely used. Kick out blocking is almost always used when a run off-tackle is required.

Rule blocking is used on the power kickout plays. The line downblocks and the lead back blocks the defensive end, and a freeze technique coordination is used with the ball carrier. As shown in Diagrams 7-7 to 7-9, call blocking can be used to downblock on the various alignments.

POWER PLAY ACTION PASSES

Although most people do not consider play action passes as part of the run game, teaching it as such helps to coordinate the play action pass to the run game. By practicing the play action passes as an extention either of the power, sweep or counter series, the players achieve a greater degree of conceptual understanding and execution. Play action passes are usually performed in a separate portion of practice rather than in the run game period. As a result, play action passes are often a poor facsimile of the run play, from which they should have developed. Once these attacks are combined in the unit portion of the practice, a greater consistency and coordination of the running and play action passes occurs. Through this method, players can understand the similarity of plays and how important their correlation is in the overall effectiveness both of the running and play action pass game.

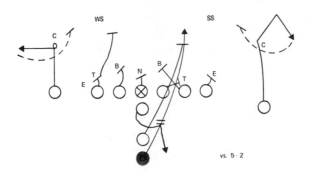

vs. 5 - 2

Diagram 7-3
"I, Power 4"
("Charlie" Call Used for Example)

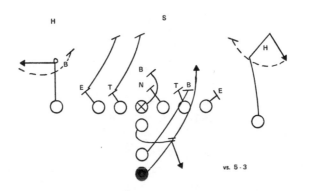

vs. 5 - 3

Diagram 7-4
"I, Power 6" ("Able" Call Used for Example—
Guard and Center Could Use "Baker" Block as Shown)

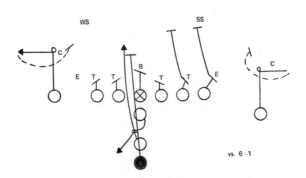

vs. 6 - 1

Diagram 7-5
"I, Power 1" ("Able" Call Used for Example)

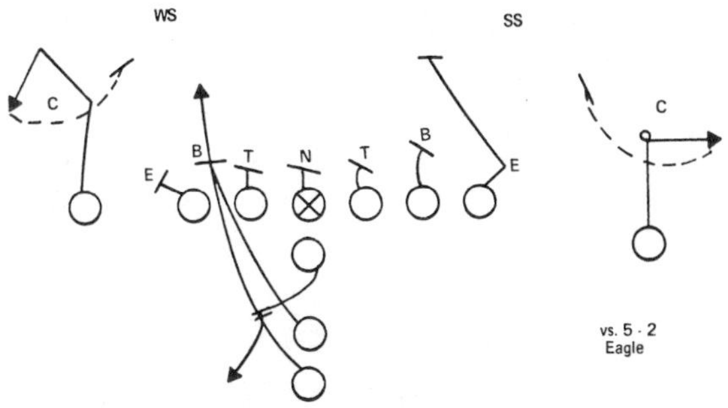

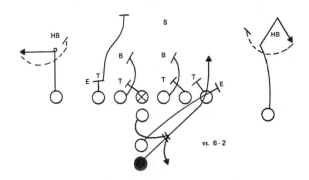

Diagram 7-6
"I, Power 3" ("Able" Call Used for Example)

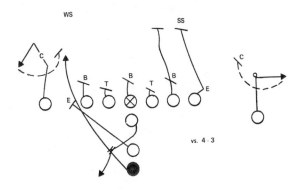

Diagram 7-7
"I, Power 6 Kickout"
("Baker" Calls Could Be Used in Downblocks as Shown)

Diagram 7-8
"I, Power 5 Kickout"

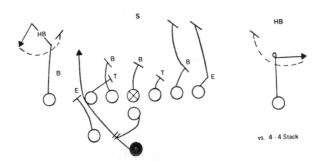

Diagram 7-9
"Blue, Power 5 Kickout" ("Baker" Call Could Be Used
as Shown to Block Stack by Guard and Tackle)

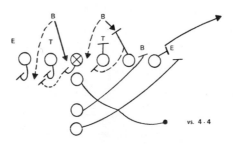

Diagram 7-10
Power Pass Play Action Blocking
To the Strong (Tight End) Side

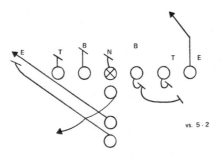

Diagram 7-11
Power Pass Play Action Blocking
To the Weak (Split End) Side

POWER PASS PLAY ACTION BLOCKING

The power pass play action blocking uses aggressive "Able" blocking to the side of the play call with normal pass blocking away from the play side call. The only variation is the assignment of the center: if the power pass is to the strong side (tight end side), he pass blocks to the split end side; if it is to the weak side, the center "Able" blocks to the play side, as Diagrams 7-10 and 7-11 illustrate.

The uncovered lineman, who has linebacker blocking responsibility, must use a "soft" technique. Initially, he fires out at the linebacker and "Able" blocks him with a butt block if he steps up to play the run fake. If the linebacker does not take the fake and drops off into pass coverage, the lineman drops back and helps block at the line of scrimmage. If the linebacker stunts behind a defensive lineman, the blocker must back behind his own offensive lineman and pick up the blitzing linebacker. This technique is shown by the right tackle in Diagram 7-10 versus the 4-4 defense.

THE POWER PASS

The power pass uses the seam theory. Three consecutive short passing zones, the flat, hook and middle, are filled with receivers.

The "I Power 6 Pass," shown in Diagram 7-12, is an extremely effective pass play, especially since it comes off one of the most effective running plays. The delay block and release of the tight end is very effective in creating run read by the Blood linebacker; thus, the tight end's release into the flat usually is left wide open. If the Blood linebacker gets into the flat area to cover the tight end due to poor faking, the scan to the post hook-up option cut of the flanker and the split end's diagonal cut into the middle short zone usually produce an open receiver—depending on the pass drop, if any, of the Mike linebacker. The Mike linebacker often is sucked in by the aggressive "Able" blocking of the onside linemen. Even if he does read "pass," he usually delays enough to prevent him from covering his pass zone effectively. At best, his pass drop only covers either the short middle zone or the hook zone, leaving one zone or the other open for exploitation. Such right to left scanning is also used versus a rotated three-deep zone coverage in which the defensive halfback covers the tight end's shute cut. The post hook-up option cut of the flanker puts additional strain on the defense since the flanker can bust on a man-to-man coverage.

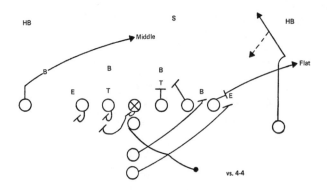

Diagram 7-12
"I, Power 6 Pass"

Onside Linemen:	"Able" block.
Offside Linemen:	Drop-Back Pass Block.
Flanker:	Post Hook-Up Option Cut.
Tight End:	Block defensive end two counts; release inside into flat area on shute cut.
Split End:	Run diagonal cut into short middle zone area.
Fullback:	Run 6-hole power and block Blood linebacker; if he goes to flat help tailback.
Tailback:	Fake 6-hole carry and block defensive end.
Quarterback:	Fake 6 hand-off to tailback; set up behind tackle and scan right to left.

The effective fake of the "I Power 6" by the fullback, tailback and quarterback is usually what makes or breaks the play action pass. Thus, the fake must maintain the freeze technique as long as possible to make the run fake look realistic and to help the quarterback conceal the ball.

The "I Power 5 Pass" and the "Blue Power 5 Pass," shown in Diagrams 7-13 and 7-14, use the same concepts described in the "I Power 6 Pass" with the exception that the halfback runs at the defensive end in a freeze technique and veers inside of him to run the shute cut into the flat. The halfback's freeze technique must be well executed so that the fullback's block is actually set up by the freeze technique fake of the halfback. It must be remembered that the fullback receives no help other than this setup of the block. The addition of the flanker's role helps the play tremendously by occupying the deep middle zone coverage with his bended post cut. He runs a bended post cut behind the safety in an effort to draw him. In addition, by breaking behind the safety, he does not

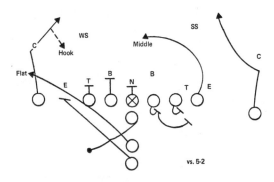

Diagram 7-13
"I, Power 5 Pass"

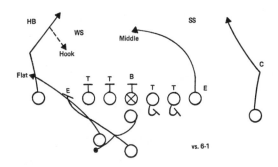

Diagram 7-14
"Blue, Power 5 Pass"

interfere with the possible post bust cut of the split end by occupying the same area. The flanker must, however, be ready for a deep post pass versus a rotated defense or a jump of the split end by the strong safety. The quarterback's read is similar to the "I Power 6" play with the exception of a left-to-right scan.

THE POWER CROSSPASS

Interesting and effective counters to both off-tackle power runs and power passes off of these runs are the power crosspasses. These cross-passes are most useful when power passes are gaining yardage effectively and the defense is overcompensating to the power and power pass side once flow direction is given. An example of this is a three-deep zone roll into the initial flow of play, leaving the off deep zone open or weakened in coverage. Another example is the common four-deep roll, leaving the off flat zone open. The "I Power 5 Crosspass" or the "Blue Power 5 Crosspass," shown in Diagrams 7-15 and 7-16, (actually the same plays from different sets) can be used to exploit both situations.

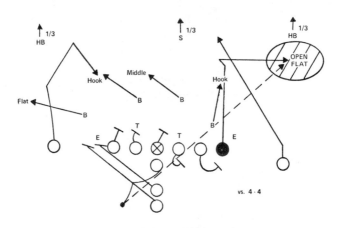

Diagram 7-15
"I, Power 5 Crosspass"
(Vs. Overload of Linebackers to Play Action Side)

Onside Linemen:	"Able" blocking.
Offside Linemen:	Drop-Back Pass Blocking.
Flanker:	Run deep ⅓ diagonal cut.
Tight End:	12 yard out cut, look for quarterback pump-up.
Split End:	Hook-up cut.
Fullback:	Fake power 5; use freeze technique and block defensive end.
Tailback:	Fake power 5; use freeze technique and help block defensive end.
Quarterback:	Fake power 5 handoff, set up over tackle and check tight end. If open in flat, throw pass. If defensive halfback comes up, pump tight end deep. If Blood to flat and defensive halfback in deep third, scan right to left.

The play, beginning exactly as the "I Power 5 Pass," breaks the tight end into the flat to exploit the open zone. The quarterback can pump him deep, as mentioned in the quarterback assignment. Diagram 7-14 shows such a pump-up versus a rotated three-deep roll.

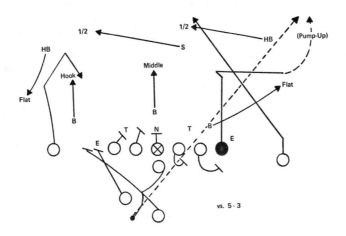

Diagram 7-16
"Blue, Power 5 Crosspass" (Vs. Rotated
Zone Leaving the Off 1/3 Zone Open)

The "I Power 6 Crosspass," shown in Diagram 7-17, is an effective play action pass off of the strong side power plays which exploits weak-side openings left by the defense. The theory of the play is also based on the fact that defenses usually try to overload the flow side and leave the backside flat open.

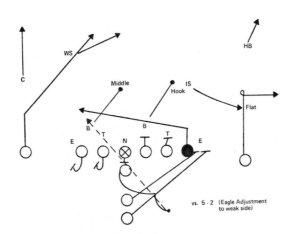

Diagram 7-17
"I, Power 6 Crosspass" (Inverted Zone
Rotation Leaving the Off Flat Open)

The play is run similar to the Power 5 Crosspasses (I or Blue) with the exception that the tight end runs a drag pattern across the formation and underneath the drop of the linebackers. The tight end's depth is approximately five to eight yards; the depth of the cut expands with distance across the formation.

8

Attacking the Corners with the Pro-Read Sweep Series

The sweep series provides an excellent means of attacking the corners simply, quickly and explosively. It enables the offense to keep in line with the offensive theory of attacking a weakened or spread-out defensive corner. The sweep series is nothing more than down-blocking action by the line with an isolation block on the defensive end by the lead back. The second back carries the ball and breaks his cut inside or outside, depending on the block of the lead back. Secondary outside-in contain force is kicked out by a pulling guard while secondary inside-out force is blocked by the wide receiver off of a fake post cut. The quarterback fakes bootleg play action away from the play. The sweeps can be run from any of three sets. The "Red, Sweep Right" play, illustrated in Diagram 8-1, is used as the example play for the series; its execution is explained in detail by position.

Diagram 8-1 also shows a combo block on the defensive tackle and the inside linebacker versus a split-six inside look. As already mentioned, call blocking may be used within rule blocking. The sweep series' rule blocking is simply to downblock with a hook or kickout block by the lead back on the fullback. However, special situations, such as the guard's inability to downblock on the inside linebacker due to the defensive tackle's alignment on the outside shoulder of the guard in this split-six look, necessitate a combo block.

The most important aspect of the sweep series is the one-on-one block of the lead back on the defensive end. Many people might think this

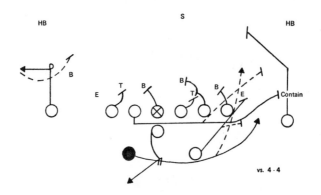

Diagram 8-1
"Red, Sweep Right"
("Combo" Call Shown for Right Guard and Right Tackle)

Tight End:	Downblock.
Onside Tackle:	Downblock. "Combo" call between tackle and guard shown.
Onside Guard:	Downblock. "Combo" block with tackle shown.
Center:	Downblock.
Offside Guard:	Pulls and blocks secondary contain.
Offside Tackle:	Seal block on defensive tackle; clip if necessary.
Flanker:	Fake post cut and block (strong) safety.
Split End:	Max-Out fake and turn in block.
Fullback:	Hook or kickout defensive end.
Halfback:	Read the block of the fullback. If the fullback hooks the defensive end, turn the corner and head upfield. Now look to cut up inside of pulling guard's block on the secondary contain. If the fullback kicks the defensive end out, cut up inside and follow lead block of pulling guard.
Quarterback:	Reverse pivot and hand-off to halfback; fake bootleg action.

is not the best way to attack a difficult blocking assignment; however, the design of the play, the speed at which the corner is attacked, plus great emphasis and concentration on practice time on the block make the play one of the most effective and explosive parts of the running game. Such emphasis requires drilling and redrilling. One might ask, "How does a 175-pound halfback take out a 230-pound defensive end?" But it can be done consistently if the block is well taught and the players are instilled with a sense of confidence that they can accomplish the block once they properly know how. Most defenses utilize some form of sit and read or a two- or three-step shuffle read across the line of scrimmage to pick up their keys and to make the proper reactions. Thus, the first few steps amount to little more than a "soft" rush or no rush at all. Now ask the backs, "Can you knock down a 230-pound dummy that isn't moving, if you have a four- or five-step headstart from an explosive stance?" They'll all nod and smile in agreement. "How about if that 230-pound dummy shuffles across the line of scrimmage with short, but unpowerful steps, still in a fairly upright position?" Again they agree they can. This is the premise of the block: the backs know who they must block and where he is located; they are convinced that if they explode at the defensive end while he is sitting or taking a soft rush trying to read his keys and ball flow, they can explode into the defensive end *before* he gets a chance to read, react and get a forceful rush into the backfield. The backs, who for the most part would rather carry the ball anyway, are convinced that the only way they won't get blown over by the defensive end is by sticking him explosively before he builds up a head of steam. Practice and repractice proves the point: it's better to get him before he gets you!

As for the hard rushing, or penetrating, defensive end, the technique also meets with great success. Exploding at the defensive end on the natural inside-out angle prevents him from readily picking up the blocking back on his initial few steps. The cut down block, therefore, is quite effective in eliminating his rush. When the back explodes from his stance, he aims his inside shoulder at the outside knee of the defensive end. The block is executed by driving down and through the knee and following up with a crab block whether or not the initial hit takes the defensive end down. This effort insures that the defensive end cannot pursue back into the play.

As mentioned in the assignment of the fullback in the "Red, Sweep right" play, the leadback has the option of hooking or kicking out the defensive end. When the lead back attacks the defensive end he has three rules to follow:

1. If the defensive end penetrates hard straight upfield or in at an angle into the backfield, cut him down with a shoulder drive block at his outside knee and follow through with a crab block until you hear the whistle.
2. If the defensive end sits or shuffles across the line of scrimmage without committing himself to a hard penetrating rush, explode at him with a drive block. Do not throw the block until your nose is in his numbers. Do not leave your feet. Once contact is made, fight to drive your head to the outside; keep your feet churning. If you knock him backwards, keep driving at him so he cannot regain his balance and drive until you hear the

whistle. If at the last second he retreats off the line of scrimmage, do not drive at him. Keep running at him until he slows down to react to the ball carrier; then stick your nose in his numbers and drive block him.

3.   If the defensive end flows outside to string the play out and allow for pursuit to help him, keep running at him until he slows down to react to the ball carrier. Once he slows down, stick your nose in his numbers and drive him to the sidelines until you hear the whistle.

The reason that the leadback's block and the play in general are so successful is the route taken by the ball carrier. After receiving either a toss pitch or hand-off from the quarterback, he breaks to the sidelines at top speed taking a slight belly of approximately a half yard into the backfield. Such a burst of speed forces the defensive end to commit himself quickly; he does not have the time to wait since the ball carrier's speed quickly puts him out of position unless he quickly reacts to the ball. Thus, the leadback can read the defensive end's reaction more quickly, enabling a quicker and firmer decision of what blocking method to use. In addition, if the defensive end uses a stringing-out technique, he is forced to widen quickly, enabling the back to have a wide gap between the down block of the tackle and the kick-out block of the defensive end by the leadback. Such a wide gap gives the ball carrier more running room once he cuts up behind the kick-out block of the leadback.

The route of the pulling guard is also determined by the block of the leadback. The pulling rules for the guards in the sweep series are simple: on sweeps to the strong side, tight end side, the weak side guard pulls and blocks the secondary contain. The only exception to this rule is versus a 5-2 defense, in which both guards can pull with the onside guard assuming the secondary contain blocking responsibility. The weak side, or off side, guard now pulls and blocks any defensive seepage or pulls up the first open gap to seal against backside defensive pursuit. On sweeps to the weak side, the weak side or onside guard never pulls, regardless of whether the defense is a 5-2 or not. Due to the lack of a tight end, the weak side guard is needed in all down-blocking assignments. Thus, the offside, or right guard, always has the pulling and secondary contain blocking responsibilities on all sweeps left.

As previously mentioned, the route of the pulling guard with secondary contain blocking responsibilities is determined by the block of the lead back. If the lead back hooks the defensive end, the pulling guard loops his pull around the lead back's block and kicks out the secondary contain. If the lead back kicks the defensive end out, the pulling guard cuts up inside of the lead back's block and acts as a lead blocker up the hole. The pulling guard still has secondary contain responsibility in this situation, but turning the sweep up inside of the leadback's kick out block of the defensive end often puts the secondary contain man out of position to take an active part in the play. This is true because of the heavy outside-in responsibility the deep back player has in helping to contain the corner. In this case, the pulling guard must cut up inside of the lead back's kick-out block of the defensive end and immediately check the secondary contain man. If he has committed himself heavily to the sweep to the outside and is out of position to participate in the play, the guard proceeds up the hole and lead blocks.

If the deep back has not committed himself heavily to the sweep and is in position to stop the ball carrier, the pulling guard fulfills his secondary contain blocking responsibilities.

Diagram 8-2 shows a different pull route for the onside guard versus a 5-2 defense than that of the offside guard versus a 4-4 defense in diagram 8-3. The reasoning is simple: as previously mentioned, the only time the onside guard is pulled is versus a 5-2 defense to the strong side. The offside guard, however, is pulled down the line of scrimmage as close to it as possible. Speed is the essential characteristic of the sweep, and therefore, the pull of the guards is not bellied. The only exception is the onside guard (right guard) versus a 5-2 defense: it is necessary to belly the right guard pull in this situation so that he is delayed a split second and at his deepened position can read the lead block. The timing of the leadback and the right guard cannot be meshed if the right guard takes a direct pull tightly down the line of scrimmage in an explosive fashion.

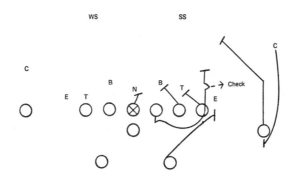

Diagram 8-2
Sweep Right, Lead Back Kickout, Cut Up Hole,
Check Secondary Contain-Out of Position to Make Tackle,
Lead Block Up Hole

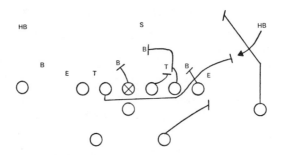

Diagram 8-3
Sweep Right, Lead Back Kickout, Cut Up Hole,
Check Secondary Contain-In Position to Make Tackle,
Block Him

The guard needs the short delay and deepened pull position to read the lead back's block properly and to take his proper pull route, either around or inside of the lead back's block.

Whenever the term "lead" block is used, whether it be the lead block of the first back in the power series, of a pulling guard in the sweep series or of a lead block in any other play series, the emphasis is always on "finding a man." Far too often a pulling guard or a lead blocking back sprints downfield as a personal escort for the ball carrier, while the ball carrier is being dragged down by a linebacker. The only person the blockers should see breaking through the secondary is the ball carrier. Blockers have the assignment of blocking; if a lead blocker goes through the assigned hole and there is no one there to block, he must find someone. His new assignment becomes to block the most dangerous man. Depending on the play, such a free lead blocker usually checks the backside first in trying to find someone to block since the onside blocking assignments are less inclined to leave free defensive personnel to pursue the ball. Finding a man to block cannot be overemphasized; this skill must be practiced in drills. A lead blocker must rotate his head from side to side, scanning the field for a pursuing linebacker or a forcing deep back.

The quarterback again reverse pivots to misdirect linebacker flow. There is a handoff pitch rule to be followed in the sweep series: in the Red (split) set, the quarterback hands the ball off either to the halfback or to the fullback before executing his play action fake. In the I or Blue (strong left) set, the quarterback toss-pitches the ball to the ball carrier. In either action, the quarterback initially must take a drop step straight back with his foot to the side of the sweep. His second step is a pivot off of the drop step, allowing the pulling guard a lane for his pull so he does not collide with the quarterback. In addition, it gives him depth to get to the handoff spot. The offside wide receiver uses a Max-Out fake to draw the deep back up and away from the play to cut down on his ability to pursue.

Diagrams 8-4 to 8-7 show the sweep run to the right and left from various sets. Each diagram shows the possible blocking schemes versus various odd and even look defenses. Live call blocking within the rule blocking is also shown.

There is the possibility that the pulling guard and the wide receiver may have to switch blocking assignments once the play develops.

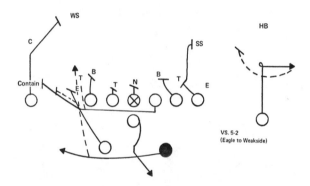

Diagram 8-4
"Red, Sweep Left"

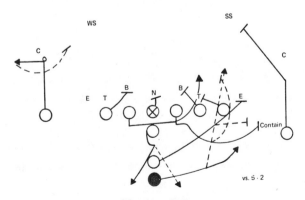

Diagram 8-5
"I, Sweep Right"

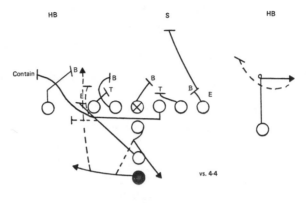

Diagram 8-6
"I, Sweep Left"

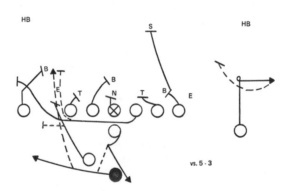

Diagram 8-7
"Blue, Sweep Left"

Diagram 8-8 shows a heavy Hero outside-in force on the sweep, which cuts off the split end's ability to block the Hero. If this occurs, the guard picks up the Hero and the split end breaks back out to pick up the secondary contain of the defensive halfback. This is not a difficult switch since the blockers are taught to pick up any sudden breakthrough by the defense immediately. The rationale for this idea is that there is little sense in having a pulling guard go downfield to block a defensive halfback if an untouched, plugging walk-away linebacker is going to tackle the ball carrier for no gain. Once he sees he can no longer block the Hero because of the Hero's walk-away linebacker's pursuit angle, the wide receiver simply breaks back out on the defensive halfback and kicks him out to the

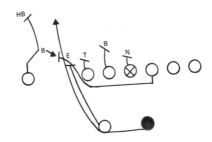

Diagram 8-8
Switch of Blocking Assignment
by Pulling Guard and Wide Receiver
Vs. Hero Force

sideline. The ball carrier, once he reads the kick out block of the lead-back, breaks his final cut off of the block of the pulling guard, who, in turn, blocks the Hero in any direction he can since the back will break his cut off of his block.

THE SWEEP PASS

The sweep play action passes employ a sweep bootleg run-pass option play by the quarterback and a sweep run-pass option by the halfback, fullback or tailback. The sweep bootleg pass, only run to the left (weak side), uses the seam theory and, as shown in the next chapter, is run almost identically to the counter pass. The reason this play and the counter pass are run only to the weak side is that a stronger defensive alignment almost always occurs to the tight end side. Fearing a quick dump pass to him, defenses are rarely willing to give coverage-and-a-half to the tight end side. Thus, the defensive alignment is not only stronger to the tight end side, but tighter to cover the threat of the tight end; and the quarterback's run-pass option is hindered by a stronger defensive formation, more possible linebacker pressure and pursuit, plus additional pass coverage strength by the strong safety. The loosened weak side defensive formation provides the quarterback with better reads and less pressure in general. The pass pattern itself is almost identical to the Power 5 passes, the main difference being in the backfield action and the quarterback's attack of the corner. Since no sweep right is run from the Blue set, the sweep bootleg pass is only run from the Red (Split) and "I" sets, as shown in Diagrams 8-9 and 8-10 respectively.

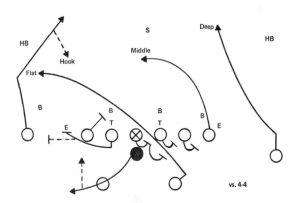

Diagram 8-9
"Red, Sweep Right Bootleg Pass"

Onside Tackle:	Downblock on defensive tackle.
Onside Guard:	Pull and block defensive end; hook or kick him out.
Offside Lineman:	"Pass block."
Split End:	Post Hook-Up Option Cut.
Tight End:	Bend into short middle zone on a circle cut.
Flanker:	Run a bended post cut behind the safety; occupy him.
Halfback:	Fake sweep right.
Fullback:	Step at defensive end as if to block him. Cut back through the center area and run shute cut into flat.
Quarterback:	Open up to halfback as if you were handing off on sweep. Sprint out and immediately read the guard's block on the defensive end. Cut up inside if guard kicks the defensive end out. Continue bootleg sprint to outside if defensive end is hooked; scan left to right. If all pass defenders have dropped off, run with the ball. If being pressured from pass defenders, read vacated area to find open receiver.

The Sweep Bootleg Pass is extremely effective when the sweep game to the strong side has been successful or when the defense begins to ignore the quarterback's bootleg fake. The guard's block on the defensive end is extremely important since there is no guard belly on his pull. By getting down the line of scrimmage as fast as possible, the guard has his best chance of taking out the defensive end. If the defensive penetrates hard, the guard simply cuts him down with a low cut-off block and goes into a crab block so he cannot regain his balance. If the defensive end stays on the line of scrimmage, the guard fires across his face and uses a

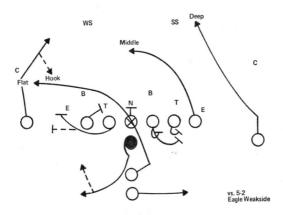

Diagram 8-10
"I, Sweep Right Bootleg Pass"

seal block; if he tries to string the play out to the side line, the guard simply uses a Butt block to drive-block him to the sideline. The guard must not leave his feet or throw his block until his nose is in the defensive end's numbers. He should keep running at the retreating defensive end until he stops to position himself for the tackle.

The quarterback's fake to the halfback is minimal; it is more important to get him outside quickly to put pressure on the defensive end. By doing so, the defensive end is forced to react quickly in helping the guard to determine how to block the defensive end. Such a quick force on the defensive end also reduces his ability to read the block of the guard and to play off of it, since he is more concerned with the sprinting quarterback. The quarterback's sprint-out aims for a point about five yards deep and a yard or two outside of the defensive end; his read on the defensive end should be made by the time he reaches that point. It is from that position that he can continue to the outside or cut upfield inside of the guard's kickout block of the defensive end. The quarterback now scans the pass coverage from left to right: if all defenders are dropping off into pass zones, the quarterback simply keeps the ball and runs. If the outside linebacker or cornerback comes up to force the run, the ball is dumped off to the fullback on the shute route in the flat. If "color" appears on the fullback, the quarterback scans to the right to see which of the three remaining zones are open. Such color on the fullback after outside linebacker or cornerback force usually means some form of deep back rotation; in this case, the quarterback should concentrate on the bust patterns of the split end and flanker. If the quarterback receives pressure from the weak side (Willie) inside linebacker, he should look to the hook-up pattern of the split end. If this occurs and "color" appears on the split end's hook-up cut, the quarterback scans further right to the tight end's circle cut in the middle short zone or the deep post bust cut of the flanker. The coverage of the split end's hook-up cut most likely would come either from the strong side (Mike) linebacker or from the strong safety, leaving either the right end or the flanker open. Diagram 8-10 shows the Sweep Right Bootleg Pass from the "I" set, versus a 5-2 defense.

The sweep run-pass option play, or Sweep Pass, shown in Diagram 8-11, is an exact mirror of the sweep with an isolation on the onside wide receiver on the safety to his side. The purpose of the play is to take advantage of any heavy secondary support by the defensive halfbacks or safeties by exploiting the deep zone areas they vacate when giving such support.

The Sweep Pass is a game-breaker type of play that, when completed, goes for a touchdown or a long gain. Again, its basic premise is to isolate and attack an over-eager secondary coming up fast and hard to stop a series of successful sweeps; the cut of the onside wide receiver is the prime cut in the series. Many teams give secondary support of the sweep from outside-in by bringing up the defensive halfback on some type of secondary relation. If the sweeps are still successful, the safety often takes it upon himself to come up earlier and give added inside-out support. The defense may even use an inverted safety roll or safety blitz for such additional support. The concept is to isolate the onside wide receiver on the safety. The wide receiver fakes his post cut and block on the safety, and the pattern is run exactly as the tight end's tight deep cut. If the safety hangs deep and does not come up to force the sweep, the wide receiver uses the "freeze" technique so that his final flag bust cut hinders the safeties' ability to cover him. The offside wide receivers' bent post cuts also freeze the safety if he stays home, leaving the flag cut wide open. If the secondary rotates and the safety stays with the flag cut, the offside wide receivers' post cut should be wide open on a bust deep. If both the defensive halfback and the safety stay deep, the ball carrier simply yells "Go!" to his pulling guard and takes off up field.

A few additional points: the guard's pull assumes a normal route; he sprints down the line of scrimmage and continues past the defensive end area for an additional two or three yards whether or not the defensive end is kicked out or hooked. The guard then bellies slightly to pass block for the ball carrier and initially checks the secondary contain to cut off any

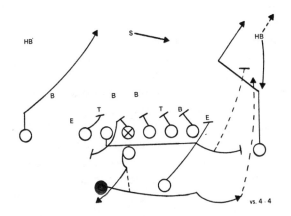

Diagram 8-11
"Red, Sweep Right Pass"

Onside Linemen:	Normal Sweep blocking.
Offside Tackle:	Seal for pulling guard.
Offside Guard:	Pull and pass block for halfback. If halfback yells "Go," release downfield and lead block.
Center:	Check offside inside linebacker for blitz; pass block to outside.
Flanker:	Fake post cut and block on safety using "freeze" technique; bust deep for flag.
Split End:	Run deep bended post pattern; occupy safety if he stays home. If he releases upon an invert force to stop sweep or rotates to deep outside ⅓, look for deep pass on bust pattern.
Fullback:	Hook or kick out defensive end; prevent his penetration at all cost.
Halfback:	Take hand-off and sprint to sidelines on normal sweep route. Once you are approximately two yards past the defensive end area, belly slightly and read the run-pass option.
Quarterback:	Hand-off to halfback; give good bootleg fake to delay offside linebackers and defensive end.

pass rush pressure. If the secondary contain does not come up quickly, the guard must check inside for any pass rush pressure. If the ball carrier yells "Go," the guard lead blocks upfield, keeping in mind his normal sweep blocking assignment of the secondary contain. The center, with the blocking responsibilities of checking the offside linebacker if uncovered, must step up first to avoid collision with the pulling guard before he pulls outside to help block the backside.

The sweeping ball carrier also plays an important role in the play: he must not show pass until he is two or three yards beyond the defensive end area. The ball carrier tucks the ball under his arm as usual and sprints for the sidelines. When he gets approximately two to three yards beyond the defensive end area, he then bellies slightly and brings himself under control either to sprint upfield or to throw a pass and read his keys. If the defensive halfback comes up, he checks the flag cut and scans left to the post cut if the flag cut is covered. If the halfback stays deep, he checks to see if the post cut is open; and if the halfback and the safety stay deep, he yells "Go!" to his guard and takes off upfield following the guard's lead blocking. In the meantime, the quarterback must execute a good bootleg fake to freeze the defensive end long enough so he cannot threaten the passer from the back side.

Diagram 8-12 shows the Sweep Pass to the weak side. It is run exactly the same with the exception of using the tight end on a deep fly clear out pattern to occupy the strong safety. The optioning ball carrier scans from left to right, keeping in mind the possibility of throwing to the tight end if the strong safety picks up the deep bent post cut of the flanker. Sweep Passes can be run from any of the three sets. The only exception is the Blue Set in which the play only can be run left, for there is no sweep right from the Blue Set. Since the Sweep Passes are run the same from all backfield sets, only one right and one left are diagrammed.

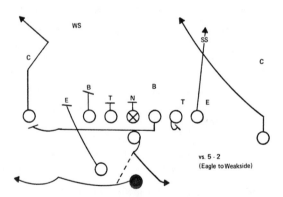

Diagram 8-12
"Blue, Sweep Left Pass"

9

Coaching the Pro-Read Option Counter Series

The counter series balances the running game by attacking any over-compensation by the defense to the power and sweep series. The counter series blends with the quick-hitting and explosive qualities of the sweep and power series by actually running the counters off of the sweep and power action. The counters also are based on the running theories of simplicity and speed plus the added dimension of disguise.

This series fakes power or sweep action to the second back and gives it to the first back on cutback action off of a lead block fake. The line blocking scheme is to trap block the first defensive lineman past the center to the backside: within this trap block rule lies the theory of the counter series. Continued success of any portion of the power or sweep series eventually leads to over-pursuit by the backside inside linebacker. This is true even of the more disciplined defenses whose backside inside linebacker's responsibility is to step at the center first on flow away to check for counter action. As the power and sweep series meet continued success, even the more disciplined linebacker has a tendency to take deeper movement toward flowside to pursue quickly. However, the backside defensive end and outside linebacker, if there is one, usually are well drilled at staying home, fearing the possible long gain of a reverse or throw-back action pass. Since the defensive tackles are more concerned with covering an area or penetrating a gap, a natural hole is thus created by the overpursuing defense between the backside defensive tackle and

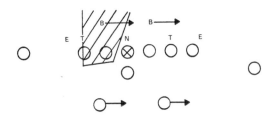

Diagram 9-1
Natural Hole Left by 5-2 Defense
Due to Overpursuit

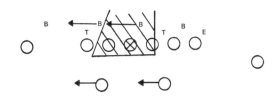

Diagram 9-2
Natural Hole Left by 4-4 Defense
Due to Overpursuit

the backside inside linebacker. Diagrams 9-1 and 9-2 show such gaps left by an overpursuing defense versus an odd and even defense.

Counter blocking, therefore, down blocks on the overpursuing defensive flow to create a wall for the counter cutback action of the ball carrier. In the meantime, the natural hole expands by setting up a trap block on the defensive tackle and kicking him out to the sideline through the trap block of the pulling guard. The offensive backfield counters are run from the Blue (strong left) and Red (split) sets only. The ball carrier is well hidden behind the offensive tackle and his distance from the quarterback enables the quarterback to fly out fast on his power or to sweep fake, further causing overpursuit by the defense. The counter is not effective from the "I" set due to the failure to force quick flow away from the counter action; the quick handoff to the up back forces the quarterback to drop straight back rather than to flow away from the counter. Thus, the offense cannot force the necessary overpursuit of the linebackers to make the play a success. In addition, the play develops much more quickly making the setup of the trap and the trap block itself very difficult to execute due to the up back's quick hitting action. To help balance the power and sweep attack from the ''I'' set, a tight end counter is added.

The counter play call in the huddle is signified by counter left or counter right. No hole is signified since the ball carrier breaks his cut into daylight off of the trap block of the pulling guard, but the trapper and ball carrier know approximately where the trap will occur by the quarterback's signal call. The first signal given by the quarterback is ''Hut'': this is a quick count signal when we want to fire out on first sound. The second signal is a number from three to eight, signifying the type of defensive line the quarterback sees. The number five signifies a five-man line and tells the pulling guard and the ball carrier that the defensive tackle to be trapped is approximately over the offensive tackle; a four signifies a four-man front with the defensive tackle approximately over the offensive guard. Thus, both the trapping guard and the ball carrier know whether the trap will occur quickly inside over the guard area versus a four-man front or will be a longer trap versus an okie tackle of a 5-2 defense. Any variations by the defense are also called by the quarterback. A ''five eagle'' call by the quarterback tells the ball carrier and trapping guard that the defensive tackle to be trapped is approximately over the offensive guard area. By approximate, it is understood that the defensive tackle is aligned approximately over the offensive guard or tackle since he could be gapped, on the outside or inside shoulder or head up. The ''Blue, Counter Right'' is used as the example play for the series, and its execution is explained in detail by position.

Diagram 9-3 shows a double-team against the outside linebacker of the 4-4 defense: he is the most dangerous man in stopping the play. If the tight end sticks the defensive end quickly, the normal reaction of the outside linebacker is to step up into the hole and initially nullify the tight end's block. This puts the outside linebacker in a poor position to pursue to the ball carrier since the offensive tackle is in a better position to wall him off.

Setting up the trap is of vital importance. The covered offensive guard or tackle slams the defensive tackle to the outside, slips off him and takes part in his designated blocking assignment. Slamming the defensive tackle to the outside, as if the offensive lineman is trying to turn him back towards the center, forces him to fight through the block, which is to the outside. Thus, the defensive tackle fights to the outside, widens the natural hole created by the overpursuing defense and sets up an easy trap block for the pulling guard, as illustrated in Diagram 9-4.

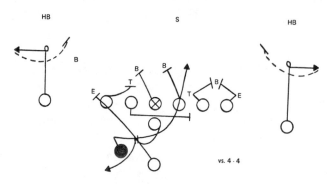

Diagram 9-3
"Blue, Counter Right"

Tight End:	Give defensive end one quick shot; double-team outside linebacker.
Onside Tackle:	Set up trap block by giving defensive tackle one quick shot; slip off him and double team outside linebacker with tight end.
Onside Guard:	Downblock.
Center:	Downblock.
Offside Guard:	Pull and trap defensive tackle.
Offside Tackle:	Seal for pulling guard; clip if necessary.
Flanker:	Max-Out fake and turn in block.
Split End:	Max-Out fake and turn in block.
Fullback:	Fake Power 5 action; block defensive end.
Halfback:	Fake Power 5 lead blocking action by stepping at defensive end. Cut back, take inside hand off from quarterback and cut up inside trap block of pulling guard and run to daylight.
Quarterback:	Reverse pivot and try to gain as much ground towards fullback as possible. Hand off to halfback and carry out play action fake.

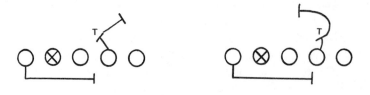

Diagram 9-4
Outside Slam Setup of Trap Block

The main exception to the setup of the trap block is versus an okie tackle in a 5-2 defense. With the okie tackle's heavy read on the offensive tackle's blocking assignment, it is better to block the okie tackle inside-out by the offensive tackle for one full count rather than to try and influence block by the tight end. Even though his fighting through the block directs him into the hole, he is slowed down long enough for the guard's trap block to be effective. This is also true due to the distance the okie tackle is out from the ball, making it a medium length trap rather than a short trap so that the okie tackle's ability to close the play down is limited, as in Diagram 9-5.

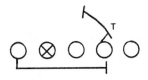

Diagram 9-5
Inside Slam Setup of Trap Block

The defensive tackle *must* be slammed to be trapped; leaving him unblocked is the best key to the defense that a trap is coming. A poor team may fall for such a setup, but the well-disciplined team probably will not.

The ball carrier also helps in setting up the trap block by stepping at the defensive end to fake sweep or power action, cutting back and taking the inside hand-off from the quarterback, and running at a point twelve to eighteen inches in front of the defensive tackle. This is done if the defensive tackle's shoulders are parallel to the line of scrimmage. The purpose of this maneuver is to force the defensive tackle to cross the line of scrimmage, further helping to set up the trap block of the pulling guard. Forcing the defensive tackle across the line of scrimmage hinders his ability to react to the ball carrier and makes the trapper's running Butt block easier.

The quarterback is not overly concerned with the power fake in the "Blue, Counter Right"; his reverse pivot and roll action toward the hand-off spot simulates the power fake enough to force defensive flow away from the counter action. The most important aspect of the quarterback's fake in forcing defensive flow is the speed with which he rolls away from the counter action. By flying out quickly, he can draw the defense to his flow action and quickly spot his ball carrier's stomach for the hand-off. All counters actually are run as quick hitting as the powers and sweeps, with the exception of the ball carrier's one-step delay. The counters are realistically designed to get the defense to take one or two extra steps toward the sweep or power fake. These steps suffice in explosively attacking the weakness left by the defense through the cutback action of the counter plays.

Diagram 9-6 shows the ''I, Counter Left'' versus a 5-2 eagle adjustment to the weakside; this is the tight end counter. As previously discussed in this chapter, a backfield counter from the ''I'' set cannot force the heavy defensive flow necessary for the counter to succeed. However, a counter action is required since the powers and sweeps from the ''I'' set are so successful. It is not so much a problem to the left (weak side) since the defense is so spread out. To the tight end side, however, the extra, or overloaded, strength of the defense necessitates a counter; and the tight-end counter provides such a counter action.

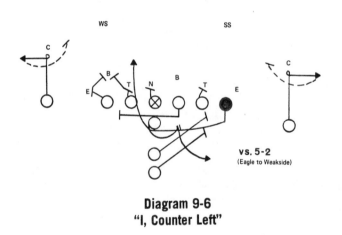

Diagram 9-6
"I, Counter Left"

The ''I, Counter Left'' is run in the same fashion as the ''Blue, Counter Right.'' The exceptions, of course, are the backfield action and the ball carrying of the tight end. The up back and the tailback must give an excellent six-hole power fake to freeze the defensive end if possible and to cause heavy flow by the inside linebacker to the power fake side. Freezing the defensive end may be difficult, especially if he is keying the tight end. Whether they are able to freeze him or not, they must explode at him and double-team him so he cannot trail the tight end and make the tackle from behind. In addition, by sprinting to the defensive end, they cause heavy flow by the onside inside linebacker, the key defensive man in the play. Since he is not blocked, he is in a key position to step up and make the tackle at the hand-off point and even to force a fumble. The play cannot be run unless the inside linebacker already has been overpursuing to the power side. A good fake by the up back and tailback insures continued overpursuit, putting the linebacker out of position to stop the play.

The only change in the quarterback's assignment is to take a flat-tened reverse pivot to put him further down the line of scrimmage and closer to it, rather than his normal deep drop into the backfield for the power hand-off. The quarterback must concentrate on locating the stomach of the tight end quickly so that a smooth hand-off can occur.

The tight end is taught to pull down the line of scrimmage as quickly as a pulling guard and with the same pulling technique. He must not belly into the backfield to avoid the defensive lineman's grasp; instead, his speed down the line of scrimmage away from the flow of the power fake is the best means of preventing such defensive interference. The tight end must concentrate on the trap block of the pulling guard on the defensive tackle and not on the hand-off from the quarterback. When he has a longer distance to cover before receiving a hand-off, the ball carrier tends to look for the ball. Such a tendency slows him down and hinders his ability to read the trap block which tells him when to cut upfield. It is the quarterback's job to make the hand-off, not the ball carrier; this is true of all run plays utilizing a hand-off. The tight end, however, must run at the outside shoulder of the defensive tackle to be trapped or at a point twelve to eighteen inches in front of him to help set up the trap block for the pulling guard.

The counters from the Red (split) set are run off of sweep action fakes. All line blocking is run the same: the only difference in the counter action is in the backfield.

Diagram 9-7 shows the "Red, Counter Left" versus a 5-2 defense. The halfback fakes sweep action, and he must execute a good fake by sprinting at top speed toward the sidelines. The purpose of his fake is to freeze the defensive end long enough so that he cannot close down on the ball carrier.

The quarterback's action is initially executed exactly as his hand-off to the sweeping back. He must take a drop step with the foot to the side of the sweep fake; he then pivots off of his drop step to face at a 180° turn toward his faking back. The ball is slightly extended to simulate the hand-off, and the third step brings around his back foot to a 270° angle. The quarterback now faces toward the sidelines and the ball carrier. As this third step is taken, the quarterback brings the ball back to his midsec-

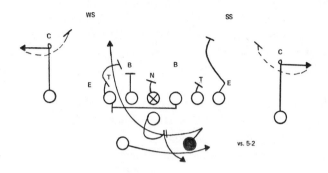

Diagram 9-7
"Red, Counter Left"

tion and looks for the ball carrier's stomach to make the hand-off. The
fourth step is taken at the ball carrier with his inside foot, as the quarterback makes the inside hand-off.

The ball carrier does not get the ball as quickly as he does in the
"Blue, Counter Right" play since that play comes off the power fake
which sees flow of the quarterback toward the ball carrier. In the counters from the "Red" sets, the counter develops from the sweep fake; the
quarterback, therefore, does not flow toward the ball carrier. As in the "I,
Counter Left," the important point here is that the ball carrier must
concentrate on the trap block on the defensive tackle; he must not look for
the ball on the hand-off from the quarterback.

Diagram 9-7 also shows a double-team block on a playside inside
linebacker. Such a double team is very effective versus a 5-2 defense: the
guard throws the post block of the double team and the tackle throws the
drive block after he sets the defensive tackle up for the trap by giving him
an influence block. The inside linebacker to the side of the sweep fake is
not blocked at all. In the 5-2 defense the flowside linebacker is quick to
pursue, while the backside linebacker is more apt to stay at home to check
for counter action. Thus, it usually is unnecessary to block the flowside
linebacker since his quick pursuit almost always removes him from the
play. Even if he can react to the counter action, the double team on the
backside is predominant enough to force him to go around the block and
to concede vital ground to make the tackle.

Diagram 9-8 shows the "Red, Counter Right" run against a 5-3
defense.

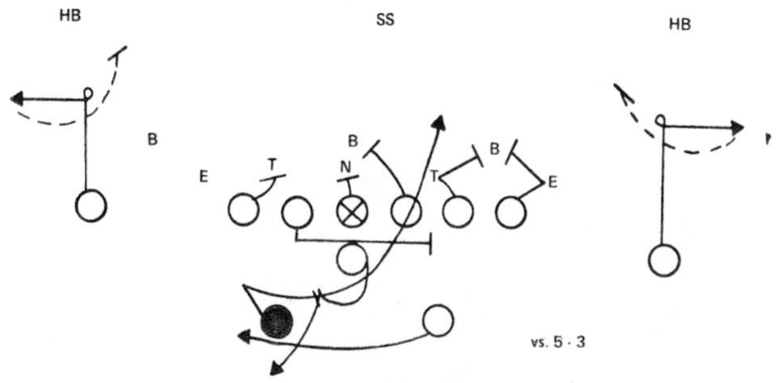

Diagram 9-8
"Red, Counter Right"

THE COUNTER PASS

The counter pass is an effective means of counteracting the defense's read of the countering back on his cutback action in the "Blue, Counter Right." Many defenses use such a keying technique to stop repeated successes of the counter. When the defense tries to do this by keeping its linebackers home to stop the counter, it becomes very vulnerable to the outside. The linebackers, with slow flow to the power fake and sprint-out action of the quarterback, cannot rush the quarterback effectively or cover their assigned pass coverage zones.

The counter pass is based on the same pass pattern theory as the Power Five passes and the "Red, Sweep Right Bootleg Pass." It uses a counter bootleg run-pass option play by the quarterback and, like the sweep bootleg pass, is run only to the left (weakside). The reason for this is exactly the same as in the sweep bootleg pass, described in Chapter 8. The counter pass also uses the seam theory: the main difference in the two plays is the backfield set and play action.

Diagram 9-9 shows the "Blue, Counter Right Pass" versus a 4-4 defense. Since the blocking schemes and pass patterns are the same as the sweep bootleg pass discussed in Chapter 8, only the different backfield action requires explanation. The shute cut into the flat area is run by the fullback. One of the main reasons for the success of the play is the fullback's role in setting up the block on the defensive end. By running a good power fake and then a good block fake, the fullback freezes the defensive end by sprinting straight at him. This helps the pulling guard to

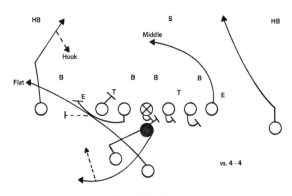

Diagram 9-9
"Blue, Counter Right Pass"

get the more desirable hook block on the defensive end, rather than having to kick the defensive end out. By hooking the defensive end, the quarterback can turn the corner and put more pressure on the secondary, who then must decide quickly whether to come up to contain the quarterback and leave a receiver open or to cover the receivers and allow the quarterback a sizeable gain on the run option.

On his counter fake action, the halfback can provide extra blocking protection against any backside pressure. Again, speed of the backfield action is the main ingredient of the faking as in the "Red, Sweep Right Bootleg Pass," rather than actual ball faking by the quarterback. This concept correlates with the theory of the play in that the defense is keying the cutback action of the counter and is not flowing quickly to the power fake to the outside. Thus, the quarterback must get outside quickly to put pressure on the defensive end and to help set up the block for the pulling guard. The quarterback's read on the defensive end and subsequent secondary reads are exactly the same as the "Red, Sweep Right Bootleg Pass."

10

Balancing the Pro-Read Option Attack: The Screen and Draw Series

The screen and draw series helps provide a total balance in the offensive attack. It complements the passing game by countering any overload of the defense in either the pass rush or the pass coverage. If the defense puts on a heavy pass rush from its front unit, screen action to one of the backs or wide receivers is used. If the pass coverage drops off quickly, especially the linebackers in an effort to get into the deep hook zones, the draw is used. Perhaps the greatest success of this series is using it as a change of pace to throw off any consistent defensive play that attempts to counter offensive tendencies. Mixing up the play selection, both running and passing, prevents the defense from finding such offensive tendencies and keeps them guessing. Of course, screens and draws are most effective when the passing game has been established successfully or when the defense has loosened its pass coverage for a long-yard down situation.

The key to the screen and draw series is to disguise the screen or draw by trying to make it look like a pass. Thus, the screen and draw plays, designed from actual pass patterns of the drop-back passing series, are disguised by having assignment responsibilities similar, if not identical, to the assignments in a normal pass play. The defense can pick up few tip-off keys that the play actually is a screen or draw rather than a pass.

Screens to the backs actually are slip or quick screens that utilize speed and field position. This technique is used rather than a long development in which the defense is drawn across the line of scrimmage to an extensive depth. Actually, slip screens to the backs give them the ball at or near the line of scrimmage with a quick developing wall of blockers to form in front of them.

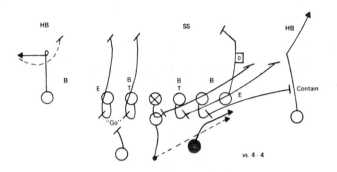

Diagram 10-1
"Red Screen Right"

Onside Linemen:	Pass block for two counts. Lineman married to defensive end is responsible for kickout of secondary contain if necessary. Other onside linemen release on a 45° angle and block first ''color'' they see.
Tight End:	Release on fly cut; you still have dump responsibilities. Block strong safety.
Offside Linemen:	Pass block until quarterback releases you with ''Go!'' call. Cut off backside secondary pursuit.
Flanker:	Run deep flag cut. Be more concerned with getting deep than setting up the flag cut. Try to force double coverage if you can.
Split End:	Max-Out fake and turn in block.
Fullback:	Release on fly cut; veer off on third step in front of line of scrimmage and look for ball immediately. Follow blockers looking to cut inside of block on secondary contain.
Halfback:	Pass block backside.
Quarterback:	Read dump to tight end. On fourth step of drop, dump ball off to fullback.

Diagram 10-1 shows the ''Red, Screen Right'' to the strong side. As previously stated, this is not a deep screen since such a screen setup by the quarterback gives the defense an excellent key. Such slow development also gives the secondary needed time to react up to the ball carrier. Instead, the theory is to dump the ball over the heads of the rushing linemen, especially the defensive end, and to quickly set up a wall of blockers to cut off secondary pursuit. This is accomplished by having the onside linemen block two quick counts and release immediately down-field on a 45° angle; on their release they must look to the inside to "find somebody to block!" As mentioned in Chapter 8, this is the key to all downfield blocking: linemen should not run downfield while the ball carrier is being tackled behind the wall of blockers. The lineman married to the defensive end slips off of him and takes a flatter and more outside route; he must block any outside-in contain from the secondary. If the secondary contain is lured deep by the wide receiver, he simply turns upfield and also looks for someone to block. Such quick release of the lineman is possible since the reception of the pass is still made behind the line of scrimmage.

The fullback must burst out of his stance as if he were on a typical fly cut. The purpose of this is to prevent any keying of a screen: the defense, especially the linebackers, must think "pass." Having the fullback block for two counts would tip off such a screen since at no other time in the drop-back series, except in the Max-Back pattern, is the fullback pass blocking to the quarterback's right side. His first step is hard with the right foot; his second step throttles down slightly, enabling him to veer off down the line of scrimmage at an approximate depth of one yard behind it. The fullback loses himself behind the block of the tackle and the release of the tight end. On his third, or veer, step with his right foot, he must immediately look up for the ball over his right, or outside shoulder. After receiving it, he must look up to read the block on the secondary outside-in contain force to determine how he should proceed upfield. From then on, it is a matter of the fullback following his blockers upfield and running for daylight.

The roles of the quarterback and tight end are extremely important: the quarterback *must* execute his normal pass drop actions. Nothing can cause the failure of a screen or draw more than a quarterback who holds the ball over his head; he might as well be yelling "screen" or "draw." He must bring the ball to his chest, stand tall and read the tight end on a dump pattern just as he would in a normal pass pattern. As a matter of fact, if the necessary yardage is ten or less and the tight end is open for a dump pass, the quarterback should dump the ball off to him and cancel the screen. The tight end should be able to get ten yards against a loosened coverage of the strong safety due to the physical mismatch and distance between the two. If the quarterback does not dump the ball off, his read of the tight end helps to simulate the normal drop-back pass action desired. The quarterback's pass to the fullback is a soft pass thrown over the heads of the pass rushers off of the quarterback's sixth step. The quarterback opens to the sidelines on his fourth step, crosses over with his left foot on the fifth step, plants his right foot on the sixth and throws the soft pass from a set position.

In the meantime, the tight end tries to get as much depth into the secondary as possible by bursting off the line of scrimmage at top speed. In this manner he either receives the dump pass at approximately seven or eight yards and must put his head down for two or three more yards or he forces the safety to loosen to keep a proper pad between the tight end and himself. Such a loosening of the coverage creates a greater distance for the safety to pursue to the ball while making the tight end's slow block assignment easier to accomplish.

Once the quarterback releases the ball to the fullback he must yell "Go!" to his backside linemen. This is their signal to release the man they are blocking and come through the middle to cut off backside secondary pursuit.

The slip screen can be run to the weakside of the formation either from the "Red" or "Blue" set. There is little difference either in the blocking schemes or in the backfield action.

In the "Red, Screen Left," shown in Diagram 10-2, the halfback steps up for two quick counts to fake a block, his normal pass responsibility from the "Red" set. The fullback stays home to cut off any inside blitz by the linebackers and to avoid giving the defense a heavy key even though he usually is in a pass route from the "Red" Set. The other times that he stays home in the "Red" set are on the draw and split screen. Thus, by staying home on the "Red, Screen Left," the fullback reduces

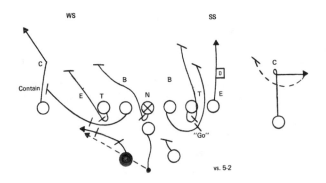

Diagram 10-2
"Red, Screen Left"

the chance of a defensive key for only a draw or a screen. The quarterback and the tight end again execute their dump assignments either to set up the screen or possibly to dump the ball off to the tight end for the necessary yardage. The tight end must try to occupy the strong safety so he cannot pursue to the screen.

The "Blue, Screen Left," shown in Diagram 10-3, is run almost identically to the "Red, Screen Left" with the exception of the roles of the fullback and halfback: the fullback steps up to the weak side of the foundation as he normally does in "Blue" set passing action, but the halfback uses the fullback technique of the "Red, Screen Right." His normal "Blue" set pass route technique is a shute cut; however, if he suddenly steps up to block for two counts from the "Blue" set, he provides the defense with a key. Thus, he must burst off his stance with his left step, throttle down on his second or right step, and veer to the sideline with his third or left step, immediately looking for the ball over his left shoulder. See Diagram 10-3.

In all of the slip screens, the release of the ball carrier should be from behind the pass rush of the defensive end.

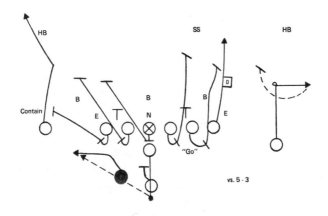

Diagram 10-3
"Blue, Screen Left"

The wide receiver screen series, or quick screen series, tries to isolate the wide receiver's speed and running ability on a defensive secondary coverage with a quick developing screen of blockers in front of him. The series is especially effective versus a loosened secondary coverage that is overcompensating for the pass.

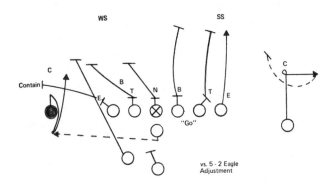

Diagram 10-4
"Blue, Split Screen"

Onside Tackle:	Aggressive fire-out blocking for one count. Release and block secondary contain if necessary.
Onside Guard:	Aggressive fire-out blocking. If man is to your outside, block one count and release. If he is head up or to inside, block two counts before releasing on 45° angle and block first "color" to appear.
Center:	Aggressive fire-out blocking for two counts. Release on 45° angle and block first "color" to appear.
Offside Linemen:	Aggressive fire-out blocking until quarterback yells "Go!" Release upfield and cut off backside secondary pursuit.
Tight End:	Release on fly cut; try to occupy the strong safety.
Split End:	Burst off line of scrimmage with right, inside foot. Cross over slightly with left foot and plant it. Push off left foot coming back behind the line of scrimmage as you face the quarterback. Immediately look for the ball—it already should be in the air. After receiving the ball, read the block on the secondary contain to determine upfield route. Follow blockers and run to daylight.
Flanker:	Max-Out fake and turn in block.
Halfback:	Burst out of stance and sprint off tail of defensive end; block first "color" that shows. You might have to veer out to pick up the secondary contain if he is coming up quickly and is endangering the development of the play.
Fullback:	Pass block to weak side.
Quarterback:	Two-step drop. Fire the pass a yard to a yard and a half behind the line of scrimmage to lead the split end, forcing him to come back behind the line of scrimmage. If "color" appears threatening a pick-off of the pass, throw it out of bounds.

The action of the halfback is extremely important: he must burst off the line of scrimmage as quickly as possible and as tight to the defensive end as he can so that he clears the route of the pass thrown to the split end. If he veers out to the sideline or is slow getting off his mark, he will interfere with the quarterback's ability to fire the pass to the split end.

The halfback and fullback on the Flanker Screen also must check the secondary contain carefully on their downfield blocking assignments. It is preferable that the tackle kick out the secondary contain if it is necessary to block him. The tackle, on his inside-out block, is often not seen by the secondary contain man, making an easier block for him. However, if the secondary contain detects the play early and comes up hard and fast, the back must turn out to the sidelines and pick him up. In this case, the tackle, once he reads this action, switches assignments with the back and turns upfield to lead block.

The split end must burst off the line of scrimmage to force the secondary to drop back a few steps, insuring his ability to make the reception and give his blockers time to get upfield in a blocking position. The wide receivers should not stand up and throw their arms into the air: this only tips off the play much like a quarterback's sticking the ball up in the air on a screen or draw. Instead, he must stay low coming off the line of scrimmage to simulate normal pass cut action. The only change comes in his second or throttle step, where his outside food becomes a plant step from which he pushes off to get his required backward motion. Slightly crossing over with the outside or plant foot makes the pushing-off movement easier. The wide receiver must turn his shoulders perpendicular to the line of scrimmage and must be sure to lock the ball into his hands. A common fault of the quick screen to the wide receiver is that he turns to look for his blockers before he really has control of the ball, and the play ends incomplete. It is *extremely* important that any incomplete pass be treated as a lateral by the wide receiver. The angle of the pass from the quarterback to the wide receiver sometimes causes the pass to become a lateral, especially on a windy day. As soon as the ball is incomplete, the wide receiver must recover it to be sure the opposition cannot recover an incomplete lateral.

The quarterback's delivery is quite similar to his Max-In delivery; the pass is made off of a two-step drop. It is very important that the quarterback step directly at the point he wants to deliver the ball to insure proper follow-through. Most incomplete passes occur because the wide receiver fails to concentrate on the ball properly or the quarterback fails to step and follow through properly on the pass.

The offensive line must aggressively fire-out block at their defenders for the required amount of time before releasing downfield on their blocking assignments. To insure getting the pass off, the backside linemen continue to block until released by the quarterback's "Go!" release signal. The center also must remain home until the "Go!" signal of the quarterback, if he is blocking a nose guard giving him problems or is exceptionally quick.

The "Red, Split Screen" is run identically to the "Blue, Split Screen" with the exception of the fullback. For this reason, it is not diagrammed. The fullback's role is the same: he stays in to help block the middle area; the only exception is his different alignment from the split set as to his tandem set (stacked behind the quarterback) in the "Blue" set.

The "Red, Flanker Screen" is the mirror of the Split Screen with the exception of the roles of the fullback and the tight end. Diagram 10-5 shows the important role of the tight end: he must burst off the line of scrimmage and sprint as fast as possible to force a retreat by the strong safety. He occupies the safety and then blocks him using a slow block technique.

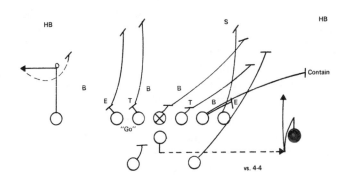

Diagram 10-5
"Red, Flank Screen"

The fullback must read the action of the defensive end. If the defensive end closes to meet the block of the tackle, he slides off the defensive end's tail to take on his downfield blocking responsibilities. If the defensive end widens, he must cut in behind the block of the offensive tackle, still bursting out of his stance to clear the path of the quarterback's pass. Scouting reports and the alignment of the defensive end usually tell the fullback which way to break his route. Whichever route he does take, he still must check the possible switch blocking assignment on the secondary contain with the tackle if the secondary contain comes up hard and fast to threaten the play.

Game after game, the most consistent and successful ground gainers are the draws, designed to exploit defensive weaknesses left by fast pass drops by the linebackers. A successful pass game forces such quick drops by the linebackers helping the draws to be so effective, as shown in Diagram 10-6.

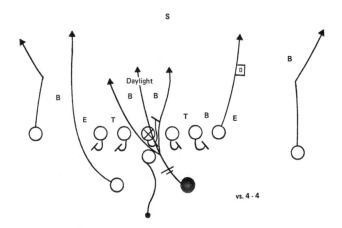

Diagram 10-6
"Red, Draw"

Tackles:	Marriage pass blocking. Lane block to outside if uncovered. Maintain inside-out position and ride pass rusher out to sideline.
Left Guard:	If covered, you are married. Butt rusher once and then take him wherever he wants to go. If uncovered, drop immediately to outside. Pick up the first defensive lineman beyond the offensive tackle's man; ride him out to the sidelines.
Right Guard:	If covered, you are married. Butt block rusher once and then take him wherever he wants to go. If uncovered, you are married to the Mike linebacker. Drop into your pass blocking stance for two counts, then block linebacker wherever he wants to go.
Center:	If covered, you are married. Butt block rusher once and then take him wherever he wants to go. If uncovered, you are married to the Mike linebacker. Drop into your pass blocking stance for two counts, then block the linebacker wherever he wants to go.
Tight End:	Run fly cut and occupy the strong safety; you have dump responsibilities.

Wide Receivers:	Run a deep flag cut. Be more concerned with getting deep than setting up the flag cut. Try to force double coverage if you can.
Halfback:	Run alley-fly cut. Occupy the Willie linebacker in the short hook zone.
Fullback:	Set up in pass block stance for two counts. At the end of the second count form a pouch with your arms to receive the ball from the quarterback. Keep eyes on blocking to see daylight develop; once ball is placed in your pouch, run to daylight.
Quarterback:	Read dump pass. If tight end is open and necessary yardage is ten yards or less, dump ball to tight end. If no dump, open on fourth step and place ball in fullback's pouch. Continue pass drop setup.

The key to the execution of the draws is the blocking scheme and the deep decoy pass routes of the receivers which spread the pass coverage and force it deep. The pass blocking marries the interior blockers to the defense and takes the defenders wherever they want to go. If covered by a defensive lineman, the guard or center drops back into his pass blocking stance and initially butts the pass rusher once. This is done to slow the rusher down so he cannot penetrate into the backfield and disturb the hand-off. The guards and center try to maintain a squared-up position with their shoulders square to the line of scrimmage, providing a slight change for the guards who usually drop heavily to the inside and angle themselves to the outside to maintain an inside-out position on the pass rusher. The guards still drop to the inside; however, it is not as pronounced a drop and they do not turn out to the sidelines, but maintain a parallel position to the line of scrimmage. After the initial butt, the blocker allows the rusher to choose his side for his rush, lets him get into that rush lane and drives him to the sideline of his rush. This is accomplished by using a seal block on the rusher. The blocker sets the rusher up by not blocking him until the numbers on his chest begin to disappear as he crosses the line of scrimmage. Once he is in this position, he is very vulnerable to a block from the side. The blocker simply puts his head in front of the rusher and drives him to the sideline.

If the center, or right guard is uncovered, he is married to the Mike linebacker and tries to influence the linebacker to go into a pass drop by setting up in a pass blocking stance. The blocker drops into this stance, counts quickly to two, and then goes out after the linebacker and blocks him whichever way he wants to go. If the linebacker drops off into the short hook zone, the center or tight guard walls the Mike linebacker to the outside. Sometimes this is impossible since the linebacker may read the draw prematurely; in this case, the blocker must take the linebacker any way he can.

The tackles take their normal pass blocking assignment either by marriage blocking if they are covered or by lane blocking to the outside. The same is true for the left guard if he is uncovered. The role of all blockers is to push the pass rushers out toward the sidelines by maintaining an inside-out blocking position and giving an open rush lane for the defensive end or tackle to the outside.

The receivers must try to get as much depth as possible into the secondary. All receivers must occupy important defenders in the secondary; the wide receivers must occupy the outside secondary defenders; and the tight end must occupy the strong safety. The role of the halfback is of vital importance in the effectiveness of the draw portion of the series, as will be explained in the fake draw pass. The halfback must occupy the Willie linebacker by bending his alley-fly cut up and through the short hook zone area. The Willie linebacker is not blocked; if he does not cover the alley-fly cut of the halfback, the fake draw pass is left wide open.

The quarterback-tight end dump pass assignment is also of vital importance in the execution of the draw. As previously mentioned, the better the draw is disguised as a pass play, the greater the effectiveness in influencing the linebackers to drop off into pass coverage. By having the quarterback and the tight end actually read the Mike dump, the quarterback gives an excellent pass play look. Also, if ten yards or less are needed, the ball is dumped to the tight end if a "Mike-Hot" dump read occurs.

The quarterback executes his dump read and continues his drop-back setup. On his fourth step, he opens up to the sidelines and firmly places the ball into the pouch of the fullback, who, after faking a pass block set up for two counts, creates the hand-off pouch and reads the blocking of the offensive line. The fullback's role is simply to break to daylight wherever he may find it from tackle to tackle once the ball is placed in his pouch. The quarterback continues his eight-step drop back to execute his drop-back pass fake.

Diagram 10-7, the "Blue, Draw," shows how the play is run exactly as the "Red, Draw" with the exception of the fullback's role: he steps to the strong side to take his hand-off from the quarterback, but his execution of the draw is not off of a pass block fake. Instead, he tries to hide himself behind the drop-back setup action of the quarterback for one full count. The fullback steps to the strong side of the quarterback as tightly as possible on the second count to take the hand-off from the quarterback. He does not step out to the strong side of the formation to fake a pass

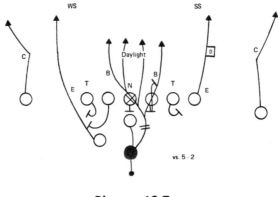

Diagram 10-7
"Blue, Draw"

block since this action does not occur in the drop-back pass series from the "Blue" set: it could tip off the play to the defense.

Another highly effective draw is the Quarterback Draw, extremely useful when both inside linebackers are dropping off fast either to get into man-to-man or zone pass coverage, leaving the middle wide open for a draw.

Diagram 10-8, the "Red, Quarterback Draw," shows that it is run quite similarly to the "Red" and "Blue" draws. The draw blocking is executed exactly the same; the only actual changes are the roles of the fullback, tight end and quarterback. Instead of a fly cut, the tight end runs an alley-fly cut; he stills tries to occupy the strong safety and influence

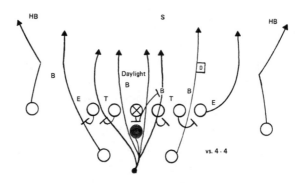

Diagram 10-8
"Red, Quarterback Draw"

strong pass drops by the linebackers. The fullback, instead of being the ball carrier, runs the fly cut with dump responsibilities.

The quarterback reads the "Mike-Hot" dump. On his fourth, or open step, he opens to the sideline, crosses over with his left foot, slides his right or back foot backwards and plants it. He then pushes off his planted back foot and runs upfield to daylight. The quarterback actually starts to read the offensive blocking once he opens up to the sidelines on his fourth step and tries to find the daylight.

The fake draw pass is a means of combating a defense that keeps its linebackers at home when they read the fullback on draw action. Basically, the fake draw pass isolates the halfback as a receiver on the only person who is not blocked on the draw—the Willie linebacker. Once the Willie linebacker does not take a strong pass drop into the short hook zone to stay at home and cover the draw, the offense fakes the draw and throws a quick pass to the halfback on his alley-fly cut. Diagram 10-9 illustrates this play versus a 4-4 defense, as in the "Red, Draw," to show the continuity of action and execution.

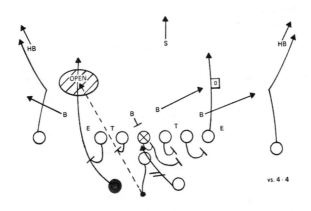

Diagram 10-9
"Red, Fake Draw Pass"

The pass blocking for the linemen is marriage all the way. The receivers' routes are run all the same except for the halfback: he must get into the short hook zone quickly since he is being isolated on the Willie linebacker. The quarterback and tight end execute their normal "Mike-Hot" dump read responsibilities, and the change in play action occurs in the quarterback-fullback exchange. The fullback fakes the hand-off and draw run; he must clamp down on the hand-off fake as if he has the ball. The fullback is responsible for the Willie linebacker. The purpose of his fake is to freeze the Willie linebacker and keep him home; if he comes up fast or blitzes, the fullback must collision him to prevent the linebacker's interference in the execution of the pass by the quarterback.

In the meantime, the quarterback fakes the draw hand-off to the fullback on the fourth step. On his fifth step he gathers the ball to his chest area and eyes the halfback, and his sixth step is a plant step off of which he throws. The quarterback must gather himself after the hand-off fake so he can fire the pass with proper follow-through.

The fake draw pass is effective even if the Hero tries to cover the halfback. The halfback, with his back to the Hero, is in an excellent position to receive the pass. It is also difficult for the Hero to cover the pass deep from his walk-away position; and with the speed of the half-back, the play usually is a big ground gainer. The fake draw is not very effective from the "Blue" set since the fullback, from his hidden posi-tion, does not help to set up the needed draw look. The "Red" set, however, openly displays the fullback in his fake pass blocking stance to help give the defense a draw read.

The screen and draw series may not seem to be the proper place for the quarterback sneak; however, in correlated theory, all plays should be taught by the same concept. Thus, the power run plays and power passes are taught together to achieve continuity of execution. The quarterback sneak is inappropriate with the run game since there is no dive series; but it is included in the screen and draw series, the rationale being that the screen and draw series is a complementary series to the passing and running attack. Since the quarterback sneak is complementary to the running game, it is included within the screen and draw series.

Diagram 10-10 shows that the "Willie," or wedge, block is an important call on the goal line. For this reason, the quarterback often calls the "Willie" blocking scheme in the huddle rather than having the line tip off the play at the line of scrimmage by making a "Willie" call. Wedge blocking is discussed fully in Chapter 11. It is important to mention here that the quarterback must put his head down and attempt to drive the center, the apex of the wedge, forward.

The backfield action attempts to draw the linebackers to the outside. The "I" and "Red" sets both split backfield flow to the outside, whereas the "Blue" set has both backs flow to the weak side since the fullback never flows to the strong side in the "Blue" set. See Diagram 10-11.

If the line call is "Able" blocking, the quarterback takes on a

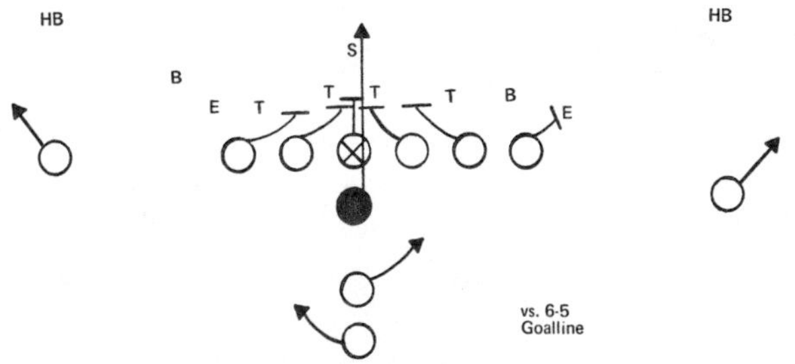

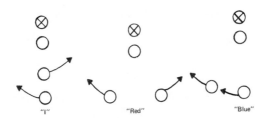

Diagram 10-10
"I, Sneak"

Offensive Linemen:	"Willie" (wedge) blocking.
Tight End:	Block out on defensive end to influence linebacker to out-side.
Wide Receivers:	Burst off line of scrimmage, veering to outside to draw secondary.
Fullback:	Fake 6 hole power.
Tailback:	Fake 5 hole power.
Quarterback:	Follow wedge.

Diagram 10-11
Backfield Flow on the Quarterback Sneak

slightly different assignment: rather than fire straight out behind the wedge line blocking, he takes a short reverse-pivot step to his right as if he were going to hand-off and immediately looks at the "Able" blocking of the line. He plants his right foot on the initial step and simply runs to daylight off of the "Able" blocking. The quick fake reverse-pivot step delays the play enough for movement to develop from the linebackers to the outside with the backfield flow. The quarterback's fake also aids such flow and gives the blocking scheme the time required to develop. The key to the "Able" blocking is to have the lineman take the defenders whichever way they want to go, and the quarterback must find daylight and run to it. Having the quarterback always step out to the right is done for simplicity, rather than having him think which side is correct. In all three backfield sets, there is always backfield flow action on the quarterback sneak to the left; on the "Blue" set, however, there is no backfield flow to the right. Thus, the quarterback's assignment is simplified by always having him step out to the right when the sneak blocking is an "Able" call.

11

Coaching the Pro-Read Option Linemen

STANCE

Any block, or blocking scheme, cannot meet consistent success unless the linemen fire out from an explosive, well-balanced stance. Such a stance enables them to explode across the line of scrimmage, to fire or pull down the line of scrimmage or to drop back into a pass blocking stance. There are two stances utilized by the offensive linemen; the pre-set and the set stance.

The pre-set stance is the quick-count stance in which the linemen block from a two-point, upright stance; linemen initially take this stance when aligning over the ball. Their feet are pointed straight and kept shoulder-width apart, but there is no stagger of the feet. This is done for alignment purposes as mentioned in Chapter 3. The linemen take their alignment and assure a straight line by lining up all their toe tops off of the front heel of the center. Once the alignment is properly taken, the linemen squat down, rest their forearms on the bottom of their thighs, clench their fists, bull their necks and look straight ahead. Their body weight is placed on the balls of their feet, with the heels slightly off the ground. Their clenched fists have a flat surface and point straight ahead. Along with the bulled neck, this action gives the linemen a well-balanced and an explosive stance from which they can fire out if a run play is desired off of a quick count. This stance is also an excellent one from which to drop back into a pass blocking stance, but it is by no means a slouched, relaxed stance: the linemen's hands cannot be placed on the knees since this causes a flat-footed stance from which an explosive block cannot be executed. The linemen must stare out straight ahead so that they can read the defensive alignment in front of them. In addition, it forces the linemen to bull their necks and arch their backs enabling the explosive, upright stance.

The linemen take their three-point set stance through an up-down movement in which they stand straight up and then take their three-point set stance; the movement is a simple one-two count movement—up, down. As a result of this movement, they occasionally draw the defense into an offsides penalty, especially early in the game or in a tense situation when the defense is overanxious.

The set stance is a three-point stance. From the two-point, pre-set stance, the lineman simply drops back the foot of his down hand to a stagger foot stance; the stagger should be no more than heel to toe. The feet must remain shoulder-width apart. The down hand is placed slightly in front of the shoulder and off the inside of the knee of the back foot, and the fingers form a bridge resting on the fingertips rather than having the body weight rest on the knuckles. Resting on the knuckles tends to put too much forward weight into the stance hindering any pulling or drop-back movement. The weight of the body should be distributed evenly on the three points of the stance; the finger bridge greatly aids such even distribution, the back body weight again placed on the balls of the feet with the heels slightly off the ground.

The free arm is flexed and held slightly above and to the side of the thigh, and the fist of the free hand is clenched. Such arm action is preferable to resting the arm casually on the thigh since it tends to create a more taunt and explosive stance. An explosive stance and take-off are paramount in effective line play.

The linemen's hips should be slightly higher than the shoulders so that the back slants slightly downward. This aids take-off and contact emphasis of out-and-up by arching the back and getting up under the shoulder pads of the defensive linemen or linebackers. The neck is bulled to block the defensive alignment's vision. Great emphasis is placed on keeping the body square to the line of scrimmage at all times and on a consistent, even balance of weight distribution in the stance. The defense must not receive any keys due to a poor stance. The offense has the advantage of knowing whether a play is a sweep or a pass, but this advantage must not be surrendered because a pulling guard leans in the direction of his pull or a tackle leans back to get into a pass blocking stance quickly.

The center's stance also employs a heel-to-toe stagger with the right foot always dropped back (right-handed snapping center). This is the most natural stance for the center in coordination wtih his snapping responsibilities.

In addition, most of the center's run-and-pass blocking assignments end up being head up or to the strong (right) side. With his right foot back, he can step out forward and to his right more easily.

The center's right hand, which delivers the ball, is aligned slightly inside of the right knee; he grips the ball by having the back of the hand facing the sidelines with the thumb across the top, front portion of the ball. The laces of the ball are placed straight up toward the sky. The left hand acts as a guide hand and is placed on the back, top left portion of the ball at approximately 10 o'clock; and the fingers of the left hand are spread to gain a firm feel on the ball. To compensate for excessive slope of his back when handling of the ball, the center places more body weight on the balls of his feet.

TAKE-OFF

An explosive stance and take-off are the keys to effective offensive line play. It has been said often that wars are won in the trenches: if the offensive line is to dominate the defensive line, it must take advantage of knowing who they have to block and what the starting count is. To insure such an advantage, the offensive line must have an explosive take-off to get into and under the shoulder pads of defensive lineman or linebacker before he has a chance to defeat the block. To get such an explosive take-off on the line, in the backfield and at the wide receiver positions, the "Step" method is used. Although the backs take off only in a forward or lateral position and the wide receivers only forward, the line still uses the "Step" method in its drop-back pass blocking action and on its pulling.

The "Step" method refers to taking off by stepping explosively in the direction the player is assigned to go. All concentration and emphasis is on the stepping out action: the lineman, back or wide receiver must plant, or dig in, his offside foot; but he must not push off or explode from the planted, or "power" foot since this gives maximum drive, but not maximum stepping distance with the lead, or "step" foot. When a player concentrates on pushing off his "power" foot, he tends to lift himself up slightly and thus takes a shorter step with the "step" foot. The secret of take-off is to cross the line of scrimmage as quickly as possible or, in the case of backs and wide receivers, to cover as much ground as possible in a given time. If an offensive player concentrates on pushing off his "power" foot and lifts himself slightly higher, he shortens his lead step anywhere from six to twelve inches. In essence, he will be six to twelve inches slower crossing the line of scrimmage in a line blocking assignment, to the hole when carrying the ball, or downfield on a pass pattern. Football is a game of inches, and this is probably more true up front in the line play than anywhere else. A twelve-inch slower step across the line of scrimmage may be all a defensive lineman needs to react to the block, defeat it and make the tackle.

When a player concentrates on a maximum step he can accomplish it only by using maximum drive off of his "power" foot. However, to get a maximum step he must have automatic maximum drive off of the "power" foot. One major difference occurs: the offensive player cannot lift up slightly when he takes a maximum step with the "step" foot. Thus, the player can cover more ground and be that much quicker to his assigned area or block. Not only can he cover more distance and be quicker, but he also is lower and in a better position to deliver a block or to lower his head and drive for extra yardage when carrying the ball. Thus, when the player concentrates on his "power" foot, he gets only maximum drive and a shortened step with the lead foot. When he concentrates on his "step" foot, he gets both maximum drive, or power, off of the planted foot as well as maximum step distance and a low, powerful body position.

A maximum step does not imply an over-extended step in which the player becomes flatfooted; it refers to the maximum amount of distance with which the lead step can be taken with the body's center of gravity still balanced on the ball of the lead foot. In other words, the weight of the body is well-balanced over the lead step with plenty of forward body lean to insure continued explosion in the desired direction.

Another great aid to an explosive take-off is keeping the elbows in tight to the body and using the elbow of the lead foot to help thrust out the "step" foot explosively. Whipping the elbow back as the lead step is taken automatically aids in its maximum thrust, and keeping the elbows in tight on both sides of the body allows the player to stay lower in a crouched position. Such action prevents lifting the body, or a standing-up action, and also prevents maximum stepping by the lead foot to slow-up the take-off and get the offensive player too high to carry out his block properly.

The center's take-off is coordinated with his snapping of the ball: he snaps it with a natural one-quarter turn of the ball so that the laces are placed upwards and across the fingertips of the quarterback's right, or upper, hand. The center takes his fire-out step as the ball is snapped; he must not overextend his initial fire-out step so that both the snap and fire-out actions are made comfortably and smoothly. The center must keep in mind that the delivery of the ball is of utmost importance. A good snap is more important than a fair block.

THE BLOCKS

1. Butt Blocks: These are the basic blocks of the running game in one form or another. The basic blocking philosophy is initially to blow the defender backwards and then slide the head to the desired side. The first concern, however, is to drive him off the line of scrimmage and to destroy the basic defensive stance, from which he attempts to defeat the lineman's block. The key to such a blocking philosophy is the one continuous motion in which contact and follow-through become one continuous and coordinated action: a "blow" through the man. The line-man does not hit explosively and then drive explosively since such action is easily defeated by a defensive lineman strong enough to lean into one heavy thrust by the offensive linemen. Instead, the lineman must explode into the defensive lineman before he has a chance to react, and in one continuous motion must drive him backwards while he is unbalanced. From this point the lineman simply drives the defensive lineman, or linebacker, until the whistle is blown, not allowing him to regain his balance.

Blocking until the whistle is blown must be highly stressed in prac-tices: to open a hole is not enough; blockers must be sure that their man does not get back into the pursuit pattern. In addition, the ultimate goal of an individual block is to drive a man backwards so far that the block interferes with the pursuit of another defensive player.

Diagram 11-1 shows the three types of Butt blocks—the Down Butt, Straight Butt and Out Butt. Basically, the Butt block explodes out and aims the nose of the blocker into the base of the defensive player's numbers. The line explodes out and up to get under the shoulder pads of the defensive player. Contact is made through a simultaneous punching-up motion of the fists and forearms as the blocker whips his arms up into a "V." As contact is made the blocker rolls his wrists and crosses them over; during this action the thumbs roll inward and downward. Thus, the blocker forms a "V" shape with his elbows and arms with his forearms at approximately a 135° angle. The rolling action of the wrists helps the blocker to raise the elbows and thus to arch the back in the proper lifting-up action up under the shoulder pads of the defensive player.

The purpose of the Butt block is to encompass the defensive player within the "V" of the arms. Contact is *not* made with the head, but

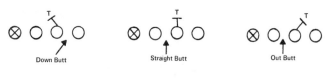

Down Butt   Straight Butt   Out Butt

Diagram 11-1
Butt Blocks

through the punching-up action of the ''V.'' Players should aim with the nose for an aiming point, not for a contact point. By aiming with the nose, the blocker squares his body to the defensive player to be blocked, enabling him to exert maximum force into his punching up of the ''V.'' The blocker aims his nose at the center of the base of the numbers on the Straight Butt block and at the near corner of the base of the numbers on the Down Butt and Out Butt. Again, the blockers should not be taught to hit with the head in any way for obvious safety reasons.

The major emphasis is to blast the man off the line of scrimmage. The blocker eventually works his head to the side of the ball carrier if he can; however, this is of secondary importance to the actual blowing of the defensive player back off the line of scrimmage.

The Butt technique is directly opposed to a Shoulder block technique, which is a slower block not allowing for maximum take-off, contact, explosion and drive. The reason for this is that an offensive lineman firing out to throw a Shoulder block tends to step slightly for position rather than directly at the man to be blocked. Such stepping for position slows the offensive lineman's quickness across the line of scrimmage. Blocking with the shoulder also does not allow the maximum explosive contact and drive that the Butt block does: this is due to a more squared-up stance of the blocker in the Butt block with a more evenly distributed body weight and power put into the block. Also, the limited blocking surface of the shoulder block has a great tendency to miss or slip off the player to be blocked.

The Butt block does eventually work into a Shoulder block after the defensive player is driven off the line of scrimmage. However, this is to cut off his pursuit by placing the head to the ball side and is not the initial emphasis of the block. Sometimes, especially in the Straight Butt block, the blocker finds it extremely difficult to work his head to the ball side. Butting a defensive lineman backwards, but towards the hole side, is an example. In this case, the blocker must continue to drive the defensive lineman backwards and across the hole, and the ball carrier must break back to daylight. By taking the defensive man in the direction he wants to go, a greater opportunity exists to expand the hole and daylight for the ball carrier. On the Down Butt and Out Butt, the blocker has an easier time working his head to the ball side. Thus, the technique of taking the defensive man where he wants to go is not as necessary.

The emphasis of the follow-through, or drive, is to make contact at the base of the numbers, to arch the back and drive up and through the man. The blocker must maintain proper foot spread as he drives so he cannot be thrown off balance.

The offensive lineman must not overextend himself or dive out after a linebacker; he should stay squared up to the linebacker in the approach, not blowing through the man until his nose is stuck into the numbers. If the linebacker retreats off the line of scrimmage, the blocker must continue to fire-out at him until the nose-in-the-numbers contact is made. In essence, he chases the man until he slows down to react to the ball carrier. The blocker must be patient and stay after such a retreating linebacker since there is little he can do when retreating. One of the basic mistakes the blocker can make in this situation is to get overanxious and to dive out or overextend his block.

If the linebacker flows to the ball as he should and the blocker cannot work his head to the ball side on the Butt block, the offensive lineman simply takes the linebacker the way he wants to go and drives him across the hole. Again, it is the ball carrier's job to run to daylight off of the blocking scheme.

2. Cut-Off Block: This block is used to cut off the hard penetration of a defensive lineman through a gap when given a down or out blocking assignment.

Diagram 11-2
The Cut-Off Block

Diagram 11-2 shows two examples of the Cut-off block. Such a hard penetration by the defensive lineman is extremely hard to stop with the Down Butt and Out Butt, especially if the defensive lineman is quick. The Cut-off block is very similar to the Down and Out Butt blocks with the exception of the take-off step and the position of the head. The blocker must explode down the line of scrimmage by taking a flat step down the line of scrimmage. All concentration again is on the lead step as a maximum step, insuring both maximum drive off of the "power" foot and the necessary quickness down the line of scrimmage. The block is made in the same manner of a Butt block, except that the head is placed immediately in front of the defensive lineman to cut off his penetration. Once such penetration is stopped, the lineman immediately whips his legs around upfield into a crab block. This will cut off any spin-out action or pursuit down the line of scrimmage by the defensive lineman. This is actually the reverse crab block.

3. Seal Block: This block is nothing more than a Reach block; the term "seal" is simply more descriptive of the total blocking assignment.

Diagram 11-3 illustrates the Seal block, which actually seals off any defensive line pursuit that may follow a pulling guard on a sweep or trap play. It is used primarily against a four- or six-man line when the pulling guard is covered by a defensive lineman and is almost always used by the tackle when sealing for the guard. However, a blocking scheme occasionally may necessitate its use from the rest of the offensive linemen.

Diagram 11-3
The Seal Block

The Seal block is initially made by taking a flat step down the line of scrimmage at approximately a 60° angle. The same explosive "step" method is used: the offensive line now fires across the face of the defensive lineman, throwing his off-side arm and elbow tightly across the defensive lineman in a raking fashion. The arm, bent and held tautly with the fist clenched, must be driven across the body to get the elbow past the defensive lineman. The outside knee is brought up into the crotch area of the defensive lineman until it makes contact with his far inside thigh, which should act as a break to stop the forward motion of the inside leg. When the leg motion is stopped, the blocker's body is locked in tightly to the body of the defensive lineman. The blocker now attempts to take the inside elbow, which he has driven past the body of the defensive lineman, and to bring it down on the back of the knee, attempting to collapse it.

This is not a holding technique, rather a driving down of the elbow on the back of the knee attempting to tightly crab block the defensive lineman back away from the play. Once the knee collapses, the lineman drives back on all fours, keeping the trunk of his body tightly against the defensive lineman. He must not allow him to regain his balance.

4. Cross Block: This is the "Charlie" call in which the outside lineman down blocks first to the inside, and the inside lineman steps behind him to kick out a defensive lineman to the outside. There is the possibility of cross blocking a linebacker-lineman combination; however, other blocking schemes are more suitable to blocking such defensive alignments.

The cross block, shown in Diagram 11-4, initially has the outside lineman fire down to the inside using a Down Butt block technique. The inside lineman steps out down the line of scrimmage with his first step at a 60° angle: this is enough of a delay and angle to allow the outside lineman to fire past him without slowing down his own momentum. It also puts him in a hide position behind the outside lineman's down block, enabling him to set up his Out Butt block on the defensive lineman. A variation may result if the outside defensive lineman penetrates across the line of scrimmage. In this case, the inside offensive lineman uses a Cut-off block and goes into an immediate crab block.

Diagram 11-4
The Cross Block ("Charlie" Call)

The cross block requires excellent timing between the two blockers and constant drilling for speed and execution. The important aspect is the explosive fire-out of the outside blocker: if he is slow getting off the line of scrimmage, he forces the inside blocker to lift, or to stand up slightly when delaying to go behind him. The only delay the inside blocker should be forced to make is his flat step down the line of scrimmage.

5. Fold Block: This block is the "Baker" call, in which a stacked defensive alignment is blocked. In the fold block, the uncovered offensive lineman to the side of the hole down- or out-blocks on the defensive lineman in the stack. The covered offensive lineman loops around the down- or out-block and blocks the linebacker in the same direction as the block on the defensive lineman. If the stack is in the hole gap the ball carrier is running, the outside lineman automatically down-blocks on the defensive lineman first. These schemes are shown in Diagram 11-5.

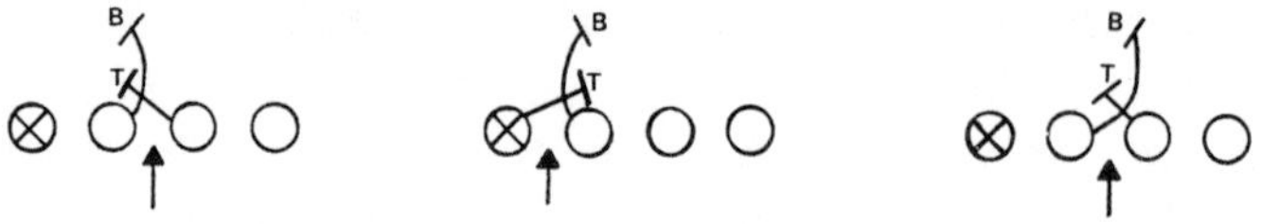

Diagram 11-5
The Fold Block ("Baker" Call)

The lineman down- or out-blocking the defensive lineman uses a Down or Out Butt blocking technique. The second lineman initially steps down the line of scrimmage in the same way he would on a cross block or seal block. On his second step, however, he drops his near shoulder and arm and steps upfield, snugly passing the block of the first lineman. Dropping the near arm and shoulder helps him turn upfield without flowing down the line of scrimmage; he must remain tight to the block of the first man so he does not leave a gap for the linebacker to penetrate. This is shown in Diagram 11-6.

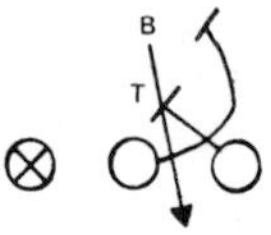

Diagram 11-6
Second Lineman's Loop is Too Wide—
Gap is Left Open for Linebacker to Penetrate

Once the second lineman turns upfield, he Down- or Out-Butt blocks the linebacker back in the same direction of the first lineman's block. Again, the emphasis of the Butt block is to drive the man back off the line of scrimmage: as he loops around the first block, the linebacker should be driven back in the direction of the first lineman's block. If the linebacker flows across the hole, the linemen either must block him straight back or must blow him across the hole depending on the movement of the linebacker. If for some reason the linebacker flows in the opposite direction either through taking a fake or on a stunt, the second lineman just continues upfield with the new assignment of finding someone to block. Such a stunt usually means the defensive lineman is dealing in the opposite direction of the linebacker. For this reason, it is extremely important for the first lineman to take off explosively on his Down or Out Butt block to stop any penetration or looping action of the defensive lineman to hinder the execution of the fold block.

6. Combo Block: This is a means of blocking the inside split-six linebacker look in which it is too difficult for the guard to "Able" (straight on) block the inside linebacker. The Combo block is a call block designated by the "Combo" call. For this reason it is important for the offense to "dummie" the "Combo" call heavily versus a split-6 defense or a 4-4 defense with a split-6 look inside. Actually, the Combo block can also be used by the tight end and tackle as versus a 5-2 defense or the guard and center as versus a 6-5 defense.

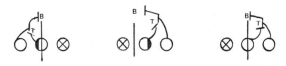

Diagram 11-7
"Combo" Blocking Vs. Split-6 Inside Looks

Diagram 11-8
"Able" Blocking Versus Double Gap
Alignment of Linebacker and Tackle

Combo blocking is usually not required when the linebacker and the defensive tackle are both in their respective gaps since the tackle and guard both have good down block angles. However, if the defensive tackle is lined up on the outside shoulder of the guard, if the linebacker is head up on the guard, or if there is a combination of both as shown in Diagram 11-7, the Combo block is needed. See Diagram 11-18.

The Combo block is a form of a reach block in which the tackle slams the defensive tackle to help the guard Butt block the outside base of the defensive tackle's number to drive him back toward the center of the formation. Realistically, the guard cannot turn the defensive tackle back toward the center of the formation; but he should Butt block the defensive tackle, slide his head to the outside and cut off the outside pursuit of the defensive tackle as he drives the defensive tackle backwards.

The tackle's slam is a one-shot Butt block in which the upper arm area of the defensive tackle is the aiming point. Such a high aiming point is achieved by standing the defensive tackle up to set him up for the guard's Butt block. The tackle must slide his head to the outside quickly so he can slide off the defensive tackle easily and Butt block the linebacker down the line of scrimmage. Actual contact is made by the upper arm of the tackle and not the shoulder. As the tackle jolts the defensive tackle, he lets his arm go loose so he can slip the tackle to make the Butt block on the linebacker. Contact with the shoulder will often hinder the slipping off action by getting in the way.

The aiming point of the guard is the middle of the base of the defensive tackle's numbers. Such an aiming point ends up having the guard Butt block the outside base of the defensive tackle's numbers once the tackle slams the defensive tackle. Such action gives the guard an outside position on the tackle and easily helps him work his head to the outside to cut off the defensive tackle's outside pursuit. Again, the guard is more concerned with driving the defensive tackle off the line of scrimmage than with turning him back. He must be sure to fire-out explosively into his Butt block rather than to do any lateral stepping for position to throw a shoulder block. (Again, such Combo blocking can be utilized by the tight end and tackle and the guard and center.)

7. Double Team: This is the "Dog" call. Although it is preferable not to block a defensive player with two people, there are times that it is necessary to double-team an exceptional player. Also, a defensive alignment may free an offensive blocker and make it desirable to blast a defensive player out of an area and to widen the daylight for the ball carrier. See Diagram 11-9.

Diagram 11-9
The Double Team Block ("Dog" Call)

The Double Team block uses the post-drive technique. The post man, or furthest man from the hole, sets up the block by slamming the defensive lineman with a high Butt block. The aiming point is halfway up the defensive lineman's numbers. This is higher than the normal Straight Butt block in an attempt to stand the defensive lineman up. The post man is not trying to blow the defensive lineman backwards; instead, he tries to give the defensive lineman a violent slam to nullify his forward charge and set up the drive man's Down or Out Butt block.

The drive man simply Down- or Out-Butt blocks. Upon contact, he must slide his head to the outside so the defensive lineman cannot spin out. Once the drive man makes contact, the two linemen must work their rear ends together as they drive the defensive lineman down the line of scrimmage so he cannot split the two blockers due to a gap left between them. Since two blockers are expended on one man, their block must blast the defensive off and down the line of scrimmage so far that they interfere with the pursuit of other members of the defense.

8. Wedge Block: This block is the "Willie" call, used against a defense that is overloading for a short yardage run situation or when the linemen are confused as to how to block a hole. There is a simple rule: when in doubt, call "Willie!" Since the "Willie" call is a multiple answer call, it is faked on many pass and rule blocking plays. The Wedge blocking scheme is also often called in the huddle on short yardage plays and other "dummie" line calls are made at the line of scrimmage so that the play and hole are not tipped off. See Diagram 11-10.

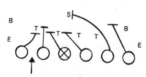

Diagram 11-10
The Wedge Block Vs. a
Short Yardage Defense ("Willie" Call)

On the Wedge block, the inside blocker of the hole to be run becomes the apex of the wedge. The apex blocker simply fires out and Straight-Butt blocks whether there is a man head up on him or not. The linemen on both sides of him drive their inside shoulders into his armpits and attempt to drive the apex blocker straight forward as if driving a wedge. If there are second flanking linemen outside of the apex blocker, they too close down and drive their inside shoulder into the outside armpit of the lineman to their inside. Blockers in the wedge must drive out and up by arching their backs. A major fault of wedge blocking is to drive out with the head downward, causing the wedge to blast out for a few yards and into the ground. The blockers in the wedge must continue driving until the whistle is blown; if the wedge breaks down, the individual blocker must Butt block any defensive player with whom he makes contact.

Any lineman beyond the two flanking linemen of the apex block usually cannot close down quickly enough to become a contributor to the wedge: this could be only a tackle or the tight end. For these offensive linemen, the rule is to close down in front of the wedge and Butt block any flowing linebackers or secondary men across the formation.

9. Pulling: Blocking on the pulling technique is utilized by guards in the sweep series and in the bootleg series to the weak side. In the sweep series, the off guard pulls and blocks the secondary contain. The only exception is versus a straight 5-2 defense, when both guards are pulled with the lead guard blocking the secondary contain and the off guard blocking seepage or the sealing of backside linebacker flow, as shown in Diagram 11-11.

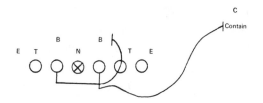

Diagram 11-11
Pulling Guard Blocking Technique
Vs. a 5-2 Defense

The pulling technique utilizes the "step" method, and all concentration is made on the "Step" foot. The guard fires straight down the line of scrimmage by stepping straight down with the lead foot. With the exception of the onside guard versus a 5-2 defense, the guard does not belly off of the line of scrimmage. If the onside guard does pull, he must belly to a depth of approximately one yard to allow time to read the block of the leadback on the defensive end. The quickest way for the guard to pull out and get down the line of scrimmage is to whip his elbow back as he tries to explode his "step" foot down the line of scrimmage. In the whipping action of the elbow, he must bring the elbow in tight to insure a tightly packed, low stance. If he whips the elbow out and up into the air, it forces him to stand and hinders his ability to take a maximum step down the line of scrimmage with his "step" foot. In the same line, if the guard concentrates on pushing off of his planted, or "power" foot, he also tends not to stay low and not to get a maximum step down the line of scrimmage.

The blocking technique on the secondary contain man is a Downfield Butt block to kick the man out to the sidelines. The Downfield Butt block is similar to the Butt blocking for a linebacker: the guard must explode out at the cornerback, or defensive halfback, at maximum speed; however, as he approaches the defensive player to make contact, he must bring himself under control and widen his base to aim his nose at the middle of the base of the defensive player's numbers. When blocking a secondary man downfield, the block almost becomes a "Stalk," or slow block, in that the guard slides his block up the numbers of the man with more of an emphasis on maintaining body position between the defender and the ball carrier than trying to drive him out to the sidelines. This is especially true if the secondary man is trying to play a "cat-and-mouse" game to string the play out while waiting for help from the defensive pursuit.

If the secondary contain man comes up hard and fast, the guard then is more interested in making contact in the more normal action of a Straight Butt block and tries to drive him to the sidelines. The guard should deliver a more normal Butt block in this situation because the forcing secondary contain man is more interested in "torpedoing" for the ball carrier than in defending himself from the kick-out block of the guard.

As explained in Chapter 8, the pulling guard must read the block of the lead back on the defensive end to see if he must cut his pull up inside of the kick-out block on the defensive end or whether he should cut around the lead back's hook block. If the guard cuts up inside of the kick-out block, he checks to see if the secondary contain man is out of position to get back into a pursuit lane: this occurs if the secondary contain man has come up too far.

Diagram 11-12 illustrates such a check responsibility of the pulling guard when he has to cut up inside of a kick-out block on the defensive end. If the pulling sees the secondary contain man is out of position, he scans to the inside to pick up the first threatening "color" he sees.

When the offside guard pulls versus a 5-2 two defense, he does not have secondary contain blocking responsibility, but first has seepage blocking responsibility. Seepage refers to any defensive player who penetrates across the line of scrimmage in front of his face, threatening the ball carrier before he ever gets to the corner. If this occurs, he either must cut the defensive player down with a low Cut-off block or, if the

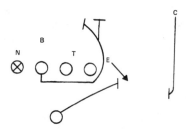

Diagram 11-12
Pulling Guard Checks Secondary Contain Man
On Sweep-Out of Position-Scan to Inside
to Find Someone to Block

defensive player penetrates quickly making the Cut-off block impossible, he must clip him. If no seepage occurs, the offside guard cuts up the first open gap in the line by dropping his inside arm and shoulder and seals off the first backside defensive flow to appear.

When the backside guard pulls on bootleg action to block the defensive end, he uses a Butt block if the defensive tries to string the play out. If the defensive end penetrates across the line of scrimmage, the guard cuts him down with a low cut-off block; if the defensive end hangs on the line of scrimmage, the guard fires across his face and throws a seal block.

10. Trap Blocking: This block is used in the counter series. It is a rule block in which the guard to the side of the power fake pulls and traps the first-down lineman beyond the center, as illustrated in Diagram 11-13.

The trapping guard utilizes the same "step" method technique that he uses when he pulls; he concentrates on an explosive lead step and the whipping back of the elbow. However, there is one major difference: rather than stepping straight down the line of scrimmage to get to the

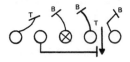

Diagram 11-13
Trap Blocking Vs. a 4-4 Defense

corner quickly, the guard initially steps back at a 135° angle and plants his foot, called "stepping in the bucket." This is done so the positioning of the defensive tackle can be read. There are four basic things the defensive tackle can do: he can take the influence block bait and fight across the line of scrimmage to the outside; he can penetrate straight across the line of scrimmage; he can close down into the trapper; or he can hang right in the hole in his original alignment. By "stepping in the bucket," the guard delays himself a split second, giving him both the time and position to read the reaction of the defensive tackle. Therefore, the guard can utilize the "step" method on his second step to take a direct route to the defensive tackle to deliver a Butt block. The guard must work his head to the inside to seal the defensive tackle off from the ball carrier.

If the guard does not take a "step in the bucket" but flies out down the line of scrimmage, he risks running past the closing defensive lineman or making it very difficult for himself to cut back up the hole and dig the defensive tackle out if he sits on the line of scrimmage.

Diagram 11-14
Slam Blocking to Influence
Defensive Tackle to be Trapped

The "Slam" block by the influencing blocker (the right tackle in Diagram 11-13), is simply a quick Butt block, or slam, in which the blocker aggressively slides off the defensive tackle to continue onto his blocking assignment, as shown in Diagram 11-14. Aggressively sliding off the defensive tackle means driving off the man to the side to which you are sliding your head to help influence the defensive tackle in thinking he has beaten the block. By maintaining physical contact as he slides off, the blocker improves the influence. If the defensive tackle is to the blocker's inside, he uses a Down-Butt influence. If he is head up, he uses a Straight Butt and slide to the outside. In the case of a 5-2 Okie tackle, it is best to Slam-block him with the offensive tackle than with the tight end due to the possible close-down technique of the defensive end. In this case, the Slam block becomes more of a hold-up block in setting up the trap than an influence. Thus, the tackle holds the Slam block for a split second extra.

11. Drop-Back Pass Blocking: The individual one-on-one drop-back pass blocking technique employs the concepts of inside-out positioning, riding the pass rusher out towards the sidelines, a cut-down technique and the cut-off block. The initial movement is to take an inside-out blocking position on the defensive man the blocker is married to. This is done by taking a drop step with the inside foot and a second backwards, arching step that faces the blocker outward at a 45° angle. This inside-out positioning is to protect the quarterback from an inside rush and is an invitation for the pass rusher to take an outside rush, since an outside lane has been left open to him. Even when an uncovered lineman pulls outside immediately, or after checking a linebacker blitz, he still takes this 45° angle stance and inside-out position on the man he is married to.

The center's dropping off the line of scrimmage to get into his pass blocking stance is accomplished in a slightly different fashion: since the snap interaction between the quarterback and the center is of such vital importance, the center's forward motion should not be changed as he snaps the ball. To change the rhythm and feel of the center not going forward and the quarterback's riding him forward with his arms and hands could cause a fumble. Therefore, the center takes his normal step forward with his right foot, plants the foot and pushes off of it straight backwards. The center either takes on a noseman, if there is one on him, straight on or angles to the right to take on a possible blitz from the Mike linebacker.

The drop-back pass block stance looks much like a squared-up boxer's "peek-a-boo" stance: the feet are shoulder-width apart with the body weight balanced on the balls of the feet; the thighs are flexed tightly, ready to explode. The body is crouched down tightly ready to explode up and outward, and the elbows are held in tightly to the blocker's sides with both forearms held up and fists clenched beneath the chin. The blockers do not chop their feet since they only stop the chopping to unload on the pass rusher. Rather, they should be on the balls of their feet immediately than to risk the chance of being caught off balance while utilizing the chopping action.

Drop-back pass blocking is based on a positioning philosophy: the blockers are told that the pass rushers cannot get to the quarterback if they are standing in front of them. Even if the pass rusher is over-powering, the blocker still can cut him down and prevent him from getting to the quarterback. If they try to run around the blocker to the outside, the blockers ride them to the outside. If they cut back to the inside, they use a Cut-off block and ride them across the formation.

The initial blocking movement of the pass blocker is to maintain the inside-out position and wait until his nose is buried in the pass rusher's numbers. When this occurs, he unloads upwards and outwards much like a Slam block, driving his nose, fists and forearms up into the numbers of the pass rusher. The slamming action actually is an uncoiling of the body by arching the back up into the body of the pass rusher through an explosive extension of the legs. The blocker does not try to drive the pass rusher backwards but tries to nullify the pass rusher's forward momentum by standing him up. The blocker must not extend his forearms outward in a pushing-off motion in fear of a penalty for illegal use of hands. Once the blocker unloads and stands the rusher up or, hopefully, at least stops the rusher's forward momentum, he again drops back to the inside, angles out on a 45° angle and prepares to uncoil another Slam block.

The pass blocker continues the action as long as possible; although he is giving up ground each time he uncoils into the pass rusher and resets his stance, he buys the quarterback vital time needed to throw. If the blocker can unload into the rusher three times, it is unrealistic to believe that the pass rusher could get to the quarterback in under five seconds.

If, during any part of the uncoiling or resetting, the blocker feels he is being over-powered by the pass rusher, he drops down into a crab block and cuts the legs from under the rusher. The blocker must continue crabbing into the rusher until the whistle is blown, so that the rusher cannot regain his balance. This action must be thought of as an emergency procedure only. A premature cut-down block often can be hopped or jumped over by the pass rusher.

If the pass rusher tries to beat the blocker to the outside, the blocker allows the rusher to get to a position where the rusher's numbers are beginning to disappear. When this occurs, the blocker puts his head in front of the rusher and drives him to the sideline. If, during any time of the rush, the rusher takes an inside movement, the blocker utilizes the same Cut-off block technique by sliding the head in front of the rusher and driving the rusher across the formation and out towards the opposite sidelines. (The pass blocker could also utilize the reverse crab block during the cut-off action if he feels he is starting to lose the defender. However, it is usually preferable to stay on one's feet during a pass block due to the possible scrambling action of the quarterback and/or the need to reset oneself. When the blocker stays on his feet, he is better able to stay with the pass rusher.)

12. Play Action Pass Blocking: This differs from drop-back pass blocking to the playside only: on the playside, the offensive line fires out and aggressively Butt blocks. The linemen must slide their heads in front of the defensive linemen and linebackers to prevent any penetration. If the defensive players try to beat their blockers across the line of scrimmage, the blockers must use a Cut-off block and drive them out to the sidelines.

The uncovered linemen have slightly different assignments: they also aggressively fire out at the linebackers; however, if on the second step they see that the linebacker has not taken the run fake and is quickly dropping off into pass coverage, they must brake themselves on the third step by planting the foot of the third step and pushing back off of it to return to the line of scrimmage. As the lineman backs up, he must scan from side to side to determine where he is most needed to pick up a free defensive player or to help another lineman with a block.

If the uncovered lineman locks onto the linebacker with a Butt block, he continues to drive him as long as he can. If the linebacker, after making contact, disengages the block of the lineman and quickly drops into a pass coverage, the lineman must quickly pancake to the ground so he is not called for being illegally downfield.

13. Maximum Pass Blocking: This type of blocking, used in the Maximum Pass Series, is simply aggressive Butt blocking for the entire line. The linemen's aiming points are the belt buckles of the defensive linemen and linebackers, if they are blitzing. The purpose of the block is to prevent any defensive penetration and hit low to draw the defensive front hands down.

The uncovered linemen's assignment differs slightly from his play action pass blocking rule: in the Maximum Pass block, he takes one step at the linebacker and Butt blocks him only if he is blitzing. If he remains in his alignment, or quickly begins to drop in his pass coverage, the uncovered lineman scans to his sides to see where he can best help in the blocking scheme.

14. Reverse Crab Block: This block is actually a complementary block tacked on to all blocks. When any blocker drives a defensive player one way or the other, whether it be off a Butt, Cut-off or any other block, and the defensive player tries to spin out to get back into a proper pursuit, the blocker uses a Reverse Crab block. As soon as the blocker feels the defensive player begin to leave him, either in a spin out technique or by just sliding out the "back door," the blocker slides down to the ground and legs of the defensive player, braces himself by forming a base with his hands on the ground and whips his legs around and into the legs of retreating defensive player. The blockers must be sure that once they whip into the Reverse Crab, as in any Crab block, they must continue to crab into the defensive player so he cannot regain his balance and get into a proper pursuit of the ball carrier.

Special blocks, such as the Draw block and blocking techniques on the screens, already have been discussed thoroughly within the explanations of the play's executions.

12

Coaching Your Leader:
The Pro-Read Option Quarterback

STANCE

The quarterback's stance is unlike any other offensive player. This, of course, is due to the quarterback's role of delivering the ball either by a hand-off, pitch or pass. Rather then necessitating an explosive stance to fire out on a block or ball carrying role, the quarterback needs a stance which enables him to read the defensive alignment, drop back quickly into a passing position and stance and pivot to hand-off or pitch the ball.

The quarterback's feet are approximately hip-width apart. Referring to hip-width rather than shoulder width emphasizes a smaller spacing between the feet of the quarterback, enabling to stand taller and gather himself quickly for his drop-back and pivoting techniques. There is no staggering of the feet to enable quick pivoting motion to both sides. The quarterback's stance is slightly flat footed with the heels of the feet touching the ground; however, a greater percentage of the body weight still rests on the balls of the feet.

The hips and shoulders of the quarterback are kept square to the line of scrimmage; the knees are comfortably bent. The major emphasis of the stance is that the quarterback "stand tall." By standing as upright as possible, the quarterback can look the defense over, especially the linebackers and secondary. The quarterback's back, therefore, must be arched but not held rigid. Although this is a slightly unorthodox stance, the quarterback must try to be as comfortable as possible. Repeated use of the stance eventually leads to its feeling natural. The quarterback must be sure, however, not to slouch or hunch over the center by curving his back: this severely restricts his vision and slows his pivots and drop-back action.

The quarterback's distance from the center is determined by his hand positioning under the center. He must keep his elbows in close to his body to enable a ride of the center into the line of scrimmage on the snap. His hands are placed under the center in approximately a 135° "V." The top hand acts as the "target" hand; it is firmly pushed up against the center's crotch to let the center know where to deliver the ball, acting as a target for his delivery on the snap. Although the upper hand exerts firm pressure, the hand must be relaxed with the fingers comfortably spread. The upper hand pressure also helps the quarterback ride the center into the line of scrimmage on the snap by better feeling the center's forward movement.

The bottom hand acts as the trap hand, or stopper; it forms a "V" off of the upper hand at approximately a 135° angle. The bottom hand does not face perpendicular to the line of scrimmage, but down at the ground towards the left guard. The top knuckle of the thumb fits into the nitch of the right thumb, between the right thumb's top and bottom knuckle. The left hand's fingers also are spread and held comfortably.

RECEPTION OF THE SNAP

The center's snap must be made firmly: the ball, in the quarter-turn delivery motion of the center, must be delivered with the laces placed across the fingers of the quarterback's upper hand. As the ball hits the upper hand, the quarterback traps the ball by covering the fat middle portion with the lower hand. This trapping action is made as the quarterback rides the center's forward motion into the line of scrimmage.

The ride must be developed smoothly with an exacting and consistent performance. In practice, careful emphasis must be placed on always having the center fire out when practicing the center-quarterback exchange. Too many coaches have their quarterbacks and centers practice the snap exchange without the all-important ride of the center's forward motion. Such practice presents a totally false practice situation in that it is not at all game-like. In effect, both the quarterback and the center will be practicing an incorrect skill.

Once the ball is trapped in the quarterback's hands, it is brought to the top of the stomach area. (This is for hand-offs and pitches only; ball positioning on passing action will be discussed separately.) The quarterback must gather himself around the ball in a hunching fashion. This helps the quarterback protect the ball as he positions himself for the hand-off or pitch. It is important for the elbows to be kept in close to the body, so that they are not easily jarred by the slap of a penetrating defensive lineman.

PIVOTING MOTION

All hand-offs and pitches result from a reverse-pivot action to give a false backfield flow key. The reverse pivot is also used due to the deceptive nature of the quarterback's ability to hide the ball when his back faces the line of scrimmage on hand-offs.

The reverse pivot is taken initially by drop-stepping with the foot to the playside. A reverse "Step" method technique is used: the quarterback concentrates on exploding the drop step backwards on the snap count. The drop-step technique is used to help the quarterback get depth into the backfield and also to help him clear the path for the pulling guard on the counter and sweep series. In addition, the drop step enables the quarterback to hand the ball off deep in the backfield giving the ball carrier more time to read the blocking scheme. On inside hand-offs, and on the sweep hand-offs and pitches, the quarterback's drop step is straight back at a depth of 18" to 24" depending on the height of the quarterback. The quarterback must plant his weight on the ball of the drop-step foot. The second step is a 180° turn with the offside foot off of the planted pivot foot. The pivot action faces the quarterback, and his feet are at a complete 180° about face angle.

If the hand-off is made to the outside, the quarterback must drop-step on an angle to the side of the hand-off. The drop step will actually be shortened slightly in depth to get the outside position. The drop step again is planted so the quarterback can pivot on the ball of the foot. The second step is more than 180° to get to the hand-off point. The actual angle depends on whether the hand-off is for a guard-tackle gap run or an off-tackle run. The 180° plus angle pivot is made easy by the drop step to the outside which enables the body flow to help make a smooth pivot.

HAND-OFF AND PITCH

The hand-off used is a modified two-handed hand-off: the ball is firmly held with both hands, and the near hand is the "push" hand and the far hand is the "guide" hand. Both arms extend the ball; however, once the ball reaches the side of the ball carrier, it is pushed into the ball carrier's pouch with the "push" hand only. The "guide" hand does not enter the pouch as this may only interfere with the ball carrier's clamping action on the ball. The hand-off must be firmly made so that the ball carrier quickly feels the ball and enables the ball carrier to clamp down on it as quickly as possible.

It is the sole responsibility of the quarterback to make the hand-off; the ball carrier's job is to read the blocking scheme. The real key to the hand-off is the concentration of the quarterback: his job is to locate the hand-off pouch as quickly as possible. The quarterback must stare at the ball carrier's pouch to the point of actually attempting to see the ball hit the ball carrier's stomach on the hand-off.

The pitch to the tailback on a sweep is made in the form of a toss. The quarterback takes his normal reverse pivot step, dropping slightly to the outside, and gives a soft, but firm, toss to the tailback. He should lead the tailback by tossing to an aiming point of approximately a yard to a yard-and-a-half in front of the tailback and at the bottom of the tailback's numbers. The quarterback must not try to give a one-hand, bullet type of spiral since this is a much harder pitch to handle. The ball is almost floated out to the tailback with allowance for a natural end-of-end rotation of the ball. This is the best and easiest type of pitch for the tailback to handle on his sweep run, enabling him to receive the ball quickly on the run. In addition, the reception position quickly enables him to read the blocking scheme to determine his cut.

FAKING

Rather than execute an exaggerated type of fake after the hand-off or pitch, the quarterback simply executes his play action or bootleg fake exactly as he would perform the skills in a regular play call. Rather than hunching over and overturning the back toward the line of scrimmage as if to hide the ball on a bootleg fake, he should sprint out quickly and eye the defensive end. Exaggerated faking actions give the defense quicker keys than a simple, but quick, execution of a play action or bootleg fake on a sprint. The quarterback must be told that his role is to try to spot defensive weaknesses left by overpursuit which may later lead to a successful bootleg or play action pass play. If the defensive end is not taking the quarterback's bootleg fake, the quarterback should let his coaches know so they may call a bootleg play at a suitable time. An extremely important rule is to have the quarterback execute his fake and not look back at the ball carrier. There is no better defensive key than to have the quarterback stare at the ball carrier running up a particular hole.

DROP-BACK PASS SETUP

Two different drop-back pass setup techniques are used: the back-pedal and the half-sprint back technique. Quarterbacks are taught both techniques to allow for individuality to see which technique best fits the capabilities of the individual quarterback. It is important that the drop-back setup technique used be comfortable and quickly executed.

In both techniques, the first three steps are identical: the initial back step is always made with the left foot. The quarterback must concentrate on stepping backwards with the left foot explosively to get a maximum step and maximum push-off with the planted right foot. The ball is immediately brought up to the center of the chest. The quarterback must adjust the ball as it is brought up to the chest so that a quick dump pass may be made immediately if such a pass is dictated by the defensive movement. To read such movement, the quarterback immediately shifts his eyes to the Mike linebacker as soon as the snap is made.

The major phase used in this initial drop-back movement is the "stand tall" technique: the quarterback must gather himself around the ball and stick his chest out. Such action enables him to better see defensive movement over the rush and blocking of the linemen, as well as enabling him to throw a strong and sharp short, dump pass. The quarterback must lean backwards by arching his back slightly to gain good backward momentum in his drop.

It is very important to emphasize a tight gathering around the ball as the straight drop-back action is being made. The quarterback must not waddle from side to side since this slows his drop-back setup action down and hinders his ability to get the proper depth off the line of scrimmage.

The back-pedal technique simply continues the straight-back stepping for seven steps (may necessitate nine steps for a smaller quarterback with short strides). On his eighth step, the quarterback simply opens to the sidelines and plants his back foot acting as a brake for his backward motion. The planting action is aided by a shortened seventh step in which the quarterback brings himself under control to enable the turning and planting action to be made; the body is brought under control by cutting down on the backward lean on the seventh step.

Although the back-pedal technique is definitely the slower of the two techniques, it does give the quarterback better vision of the entire defense. His back is never turned to one side of the field as he drops back, enabling total vision all through the drop. This is an excellent technique for quarterbacks with quick feet since their drops are slowed down only slightly by such back-pedalling.

The half-sprint back technique utilizes the back pedal for three steps. This enables the quarterback to dump the ball off if the defensive movement so dictates. On the fourth step, however, the quarterback opens to the sidelines on a 90° angle. The fifth step is a cross-over step with the foot again facing the sidelines; the sixth step is a slide step with the back foot in a backwards direction, with the seventh step a repeated cross-over of the fifth step. During the second half of the sprint back action, the body still leans backwards as it faces the sideline. On the seventh step, however, the body is brought under control as the body lean is cut down. The eighth step is a plant step made exactly as the eighth step of the drop-back pedal technique. As in the back-pedal technique, a smaller quarterback with shorter strides might necessitate a ninth and tenth drop step; but this would be at the expense of speed and time.

The semi-sprint back technique is the faster of the two techniques in setting up and also blends well with the draw hand-offs. The one major drawback of the semi-sprint back technique is that the range of vision of the quarterback is severely cut down to the backside. The straight sprint-back technique is not used since it does not enable the quarterbacks to deliver the dump pass effectively.

The two-, four- and six-step drop-back setups also come off of the back-pedal technique. The difference lies in the planting of the second, fourth or sixth step: in the two-step drop back, the quarterback drop steps, pivots off the ball of the foot of the drop step and immediately plants the back foot. The only variation to this technique is that if the quarterback is opening up to the right, the second, or plant step, is made at approximately a 180° angle plus rotation. If he is opening to the left, the plant step is made at approximately a 75° angle. If the quarterback is throwing to the right on a four- or six-step drop, the setup is made like a normal eight-step drop setup. If the pass off the four- or six-step drop is made to the left, the quarterback again opens up at a 75° angle to allow the quarterback to have a balanced and comfortable stance to deliver the ball from and properly follow through on his passing action.

POWER PASS SETUP

The power pass setup is initially made like the reverse pivot hand-off technique of the power plays. The reverse pivot is made off of the outside drop step of the playside foot; the second step is the normal 180° plus turn. A hand fake is given with the inside hand as the ball is carried on the lower, outside part of the stomach. The quarterback does not carry the ball on his hip since the ball rides better on the stomach area. In addition, the quarterback can protect the ball better when receiving a blow from behind since the ball is more easily absorbed into the softness of the stomach than on the hard surface of the hip.

On the third step, the quarterback continues past the faking back on approximately a 135° angle; the ball is grasped by both hands, adjusted so the fingers grip the laces properly and brought to the middle chest area. The fourth step continues on the same course; however, the body is brought under control as body lean is cut down. The fourth step actually plants the inside foot on the ball of the foot. The fifth step is a plant step off of a slight pivot of the inside foot so that the body is squared up to the sidelines.

PASSING

An extremely important phase of passing is the grip on the ball by the throwing hand. The ball must be held with the fingertips, the thumb and the heel of the hand; it should not rest on the palm of the hand. The grip should be firm and comfortable, never squeezed. The middle of the hand must be placed on the back portion of the ball with the front three fingertips gripped to the laces. (All four fingertips could possibly be placed on the laces. This is especially true of the extra long lace ball many passing teams like to use for their quarterbacks.)

The quarterbacks do not cock the ball behind their ear as soon as they plant their back foot. Holding the ball up in the air like that is dangerous since the quarterback cannot protect it on a backside tackle. In addition, it is quite uncomfortable and actually an unnatural stance. Instead, the quarterback holds the ball comfortably in the middle of the chest.

The phrase used to describe how the ball should be thrown is "throwing darts." The technique is similar to that of a baseball catcher making a peg to second or someone throwing darts at a dartboard. Rather than the passing action taking on two distinct motions—draw the ball back and throw, the quarterbacks think of the passing action as one continuous, coordinated motion combining both. Thus, the quarterback draws the ball slightly down and back, brings it up over the ear and fires the ball on a high, over-the-head release. On the drawing back of the football, the back shoulder is actually dropped slightly to help get the necessary arching trajectory. It is important for the quarterback to cock his wrist so a wobbly pass is not thrown; the ball should come off the helmet as close as possible. As the ball is drawn back, the front arm and hand extend out in the direction of the pass to give the quarterback a sense of balance. The longer the pass has to be thrown, the greater the drop of the back shoulder and the higher the front arm and hand reach out.

Follow-through is the key to the delivery of the ball: initially, the body weight is positioned on the back foot; there is a slight bend of both knees. As the pass is thrown, the body weight is shifted to the front foot as the quarterback pushes off the back, or planted foot. It is extremely important that the front, or lead foot steps out in the direction of the pass with the toes directly aimed at the spot to which the ball is to be thrown. The back hip is whipped around with the forward motion of the passing arm.

The ball is delivered with a snap of the wrist off of the locked wrist and elbow cock of the ball. The technique looks much like an effort to throw a screwball: the thumb of the throwing hand is snapped down. The quarterback points at the aiming spot with the index finger when throwing. However, the index finger and remaining fingers also must continue their follow-through motion and end up pointing at the ground. Terms used in teaching the follow-through method are "zip!" the ball or "snap!" it off.

BOOTLEG PASSING

Bootleg passing is actually accomplished off of sprint-out action to the left. The most important technique to master in bootleg passing is throwing on the run, and the best method is a "Step-Up" technique. "Step Up" means stepping up into the line of scrimmage to get the shoulders square to the line of scrimmage. The quarterback must not throw the ball when he is facing the sidelines since he cannot follow-through properly.

If the quarterback has already cut up inside the kick out block of the defensive, he does not have to worry about planting his left foot and cutting up to the line of scrimmage to square his shoulders. The quarterback sprinting to the outside must plant his left foot and step at the line of scrimmage with his right, or inside, foot. The quarterback plants his left foot and pivots on the ball of the foot. As he pivots he steps directly at the line of scrimmage; his squaring effort is aided by a drawing back of the football to the right side of the chest. From this position the quarterback simply executes his normal passing action by pushing off the right foot and using the "throwing darts" technique. The pass, then, is thrown off of the left or front foot as the forward stepping motion is made. Since the pass is thrown with the shoulders square to the line of scrimmage, it is important for the quarterback to heavily emphasize arm follow-through.

The only exception to this technique is when the quarterback spots the split end wide open after busting deep and has plenty of time to reset to throw a long pass. If he is not being pressured by the pass rush, he simply plants his left foot and turns himself around completely in a 180° turn into his normal passing stance facing his right sideline. From this stance he carries out his normal passing technique.

DUMP PASSING

Dump passing to the "Mike-Hot" receiver is made while back-pedalling. Since the pass is made while the quarterback is going backwards, it is important that he lift himself up on the balls of his feet to gather all of his throwing power into the upper torso portion of his body. The quarterback uses the "throwing darts" technique: to get a good, short dump pass he must stick his chest out and be sure to "zip" or "snap" the ball off. Much like the bootleg passing, the quarterback must heavily emphasize arm follow-through.

The dump pass to the "Blood-Hot" receiver is made off of a normal four-step drop-back setup. If the quarterback reads "dump" to the "Blood-Hot" receiver, he simply opens on the fourth step and plants his back foot. From this stance, he carries out his normal passing technique. The quick opening step on the fourth step is a natural part of the half-sprint back setup. This is another reason the half-sprint back setup technique seems to fit better into the passing game.

PASSING IN THE RAIN

The problem of rain and a wet field is one of the greatest "knocks" on a pass-oriented offense. It is true that the wetness does not help the passing of the quarterback; however, it does not have to be anywhere near as serious a problem as it seems to be. Handling a wet ball is only a serious problem when the quarterback is not used to it. As a result, the team must practice in the rain if it is a pass-oriented team or not. Rainy day practices also should be offense-oriented with a heavy concentration on passing work. If rain is forecast for an upcoming Saturday's game, be sure to have a "Bucket Day" in practice on Thursday and Friday. During "Bucket Day" a manager dunks the practice ball in a bucket of water every two or three plays. Not only does the quarterback become used to the handling and passing of a wet ball; but the receivers and backs do as well.

13

Developing an Explosive Backfield

Two stances are utilized by the fullback and the halfback—the down, three-point stance and the upright, two-point stance. The three-point stance is almost identical to the lineman's three-point stance except that there is an even distribution of weight on the tripod. The backs need equal explosive lateral take-off ability as well as forward take-off ability. In addition, they should not be sloping down slightly as the linemen. Instead, backs should be parallel to the ground, helping to give a more even distribution of weight on the tripod. Feet must still be pointed straight ahead; the slight heel-to-toe stagger can be used. The feet should be no more than shoulder-width apart.

The down hand utilizes the finger bridge: it is placed slightly in front of the shoulder, slightly inside of the corresponding knee and an inch or two closer to the body than to the lineman to give a more even distribution of the body weight. The opposite arm and hand are cocked and clenched and held above the corresponding thigh explosively in the same manner as the linemen. The neck is bulled with the eyes focusing straight ahead using peripheral vision to view the defensive alignment.

The two-point, or upright stance is the quick-count stance and the stance for the tailback in the "I." The feet are parallel with no stagger and perpendicular to the line of scrimmage; the heels of the feet touch the ground lightly. However, most of the body weight is still placed on the balls of the feet.

The hands are placed on the upper part of the thighs. By doing this the back can arch his back properly and bull his neck to prevent a slouching stance. His eyes are focused straight ahead, just as in the three-point stance.

TAKE-OFF

Take-off for the back from either stance utilizes the "Step" method. All concentration is on stepping explosively in the desired direction to get both a maximum step and maximum drive off of the power foot.

On sweep action, the back must help himself to get explosive lateral movement by whipping back his elbow to help him get down the line of scrimmage. On the initial sweep step, the "Step" foot takes a slight belly action into the backfield by not directly stepping parallel to the line of scrimmage. Instead, the back drops his "Step" foot back approximately an extra twelve inches: this helps to get the back at a slight belly depth of an extra half-yard to a yard.

An important part of the take-off for the backs, as well as the linemen and wide receivers, is not to "open up" their body movement through excessive loose movement. Backs seem to have a tendency of standing up in a loose holding of the body, rather than a tight, low, compact stance which emulates explosive take-off and drive. To combat such excessive loose movement and standing up, the back must concentrate on keeping his elbows in as if he were going to throw a punch. Throwing the elbows outward usually results in the loose carrying of the body and the standing up approach to the line of scrimmage.

THE HAND-OFF

An important concept for the back to realize is that the hand-off is not his responsibility; it is the quarterback's role to place the ball in his pouch. The ball carrier's role is to watch the blocking scheme develop and find the daylight. The back must concentrate on exploding toward the designated hole, form his pouch and clamp down on the ball when he feels it hit his stomach.

The ball carrier forms his pouch by raising his inside elbow to the quarterback. This is best accomplished by turning the thumb of the inside hand down. The inside arm slants downward to help form a "V"-shaped pouch. The thumb and index finder should be touching the outside portion of the chest, the fingers comfortably spread and relaxed to be ready to grip the ball.

The outside arm is held across the bottom of the stomach, slanting downward to form the other part of the ''V.'' The fingers also are comfortably spread in a ready position to grasp the ball.

When the ball carrier feels the ball placed against his stomach, he simply clamps down on it. His hands and fingers wrap around the ends of the ball. We coach our backs to utilize a two-handed carry when running through the line of scrimmage on the powers and counters until they have broken past the linebackers. It is of vital importance that the back does not watch the ball being placed in his pouch: this only slows him down and prevents him from seeing the blocking scheme develop.

BALL CARRYING

As already mentioned, the backs must utilize a two-handed carry until they pass the linebackers. Once they break into daylight, or when on sweep runs, the ball is tucked under the outside arm. It is extremely important that the hand grasps the ball over the tip to lock it into the armpit.

When he explodes from his stance and takes the hand-off, his aiming point is dead center of the assigned gap. The ball carrier should penetrate the hole as quickly as possible, emphasizing speed and power. He must not hesitate to look for an opening. The back must develop the confidence that daylight will open somewhere in the gap as he approaches the line of scrimmage. The key is to have him quickly explode through that daylight at top speed. If there is no hole, he must utilize that speed and power to lower his head and grind out short yardage.

Such quick explosion into and through the line of scrimmage drastically reduces the ability of the defense to pursue. In addition, yardage is rarely lost which would create the long yardage situations; rather, steady middle yardage gains of three to seven yards are achieved, which help to maintain ball control. Players should constantly drill to break to daylight by cutting back to the inside, straight upfield or to the outside.

One major emphasis is that whatever direction the ball carrier takes, it must be ''North-South,'' always upfield towards the goal line. No matter which way the back cuts, he must be gaining yardage. A major means of accomplishing ''North-South'' running is to have the ball carrier run at a defender and cut or veer away rather than trying to cut to the inside or outside and out-run the defender. The backs sprint right at the defender to freeze him in a break-down position, while trying to determine to which direction the ball carrier is going to cut. During this ''setup'' technique, the back is always gaining ground; once he is approximately a yard and a half to two yards from the defender, he breaks to the side of the most open daylight at top speed. Such a "freeze" technique often forces the defender to become flat-footed, unable to stop the ball carrier on his quick-breaking cut or veer.

When the ball carrier tries to break or cut to the inside or outside on an "East-West" direction early, he gives the defender an excellent opportunity to have a good cut-off angle in pursuing the ball carrier. In addition, the early cut pretty much declares the direction of the ball carrier and makes it much more difficult for him to try to break back in the opposite direction if daylight develops there.

Once the ball carrier realizes he cannot cut to daylight, he should use a low, driving technique to try to run through and over the interference. This can be done utilizing two techniques: if the ball carrier is cradling the ball with two arms, he lowers his head and blasts up and through the defender(s) by arching his back and driving up and through the interference. Low, driving leg churn is of utmost importance.

If the ball carrier is utilizing a one arm carry, he uses the same low, driving arch-the-back technique. However, he uses his free shoulder as a battering ram much like a shoulder block. The back lowers his head and rips his shoulder up into the numbers of the defender to get under the defender's shoulder pads. Once he makes contact, the ball carrier utilizes the same driving technique up and through the defender, using low, driving leg churn.

If the ball carrier is running along the sidelines, it is important for him to tuck the ball under his outside arm. His free arm and shoulder must be free to ward off interference. Sideline runners should lower their inside shoulders and blast through the defenders for extra yardage rather than using a cut-back technique. Of course, if a back has exceptional speed and cutting ability, he should break back to the inside towards daylight. The average back, however, gains more yardage by lowering his shoulder than trying to cut back.

The stiff arm technique is an excellent open field weapon. The backs simply carry their free arm low and snap the heel of the free hand out at the defender's forehead. It is important that the elbow aid the snapping action by being tucked in tight to the body, so that the stiff arm is an inside-out driving action helping to put power into the snapping action of the stiff arm.

The free arm is extremely important for the use of the balance hand when the ball carrier is stumbling or falling. When the ball carrier loses his balance as he is going forward, he must stick out his arm in a stiff-arm fashion to break the fall. The hand should hit the ground flat to absorb all the body weight and to stabilize the body balance. From this position the ball carrier must push off the heel of the hand, buck the head upward and arch his back. The leg action must pump the knees high to help regain the body balance and to get back into a running stride.

Protecting the ball upon impact with a defensive player or the ground is vitally important. When the ball carrier is about to make contact with a defensive player, he must cradle the ball with both arms; the two hands should cup the tips of the ball. When the ball carrier is about to hit the ground, he must not try to extend the ball from under his chest and stomach area. Such extension often leads to fumbles since it is no longer protected by the body.

Coaching ball carriers must allow for individual styles. Some runners are naturals, but others need to be taught from the ground on up. It is very important not to over-coach the talented runner. Running "North-South" and speed must be emphasized; "jitter-bugging" and running "East-West" are the major faults to be eliminated.

FAKING

Faking the hand-off and ball carrying relies more on speed and natural play action than on exaggerated arm action and a lowering of the head. Simply clamping down with the top arm and running at top speed achieves the most deceptive fakes. In addition, keeping the head up and the eyes focused on the faking hole does much to freeze defensive players in their efforts to determine if the back has the ball or not.

Once into the hole, the back has the responsibility of collisioning the free defensive player in the faking hole area. If there is no one to collision and the back finds himself at linebacker depth, his assignment changes to finding someone to block. His first scan should be to the backside to pick up the first backside pursuit that appears.

BACKFIELD BLOCKING

For simplicity in teaching and coaching methodology, backfield blocking techniques are almost identical to line blocking techniques; the major exceptions are in the approach to the blocks or in special techniques to cut down on the advantage of a large, hard-charging defensive lineman or linebacker.

1. Sweep Block: The lead back sweep block on the end is the most difficult block to master and perhaps the most important one. If the backs cannot handle the defensive end, the sweep will simply not go, cutting out the offense's ability to attack the outside. Therefore, backs should spend much practice time on the sweep block. If there is any one block that demands excellence, it is the sweep block.

As already explained in the "Red, Sweep Right" play, the explosive attacking of the defensive end by the lead back before he has a chance to react properly to the sweep action, is the key to the block's execution. Instilling confidence in the back's ability to block the defensive ends if they explode at them is the ultimate key. If they explode out into the defensive end before he gets the opportunity to react to the play properly, forcefully and powerfully, it becomes a simple means of executing the blocking technique.

There are three basic reactions the defensive end can make when reading the sweep: he can penetrate hard across the line of scrimmage into the backfield; he can hang in his alignment area; or he can try to string the play out to the sidelines. If the defensive end penetrates hard, the back uses a modified Cut-off block. He keeps his head to the outside and aims his inside shoulder at the outside knee of the defensive end. The block is a low, hard drive that attempts to cut the defensive end's outside leg from under him. After this cut block has been thrown, the back brakes himself with his hands and immediately goes into a crab block to prevent the defensive end from regaining his balance.

If the defensive end hangs in his alignment area, the back uses a Seal block technique, identical to the lineman's Seal block technique: the inside arm and elbow are driven across the front of the defensive end tightly in a raking fashion. The forward motion is stopped by driving the inside knee into the defensive end's inside thigh. The inside elbow locks around the outside leg and drives down on the back of the knee area to collapse it. The back follows through by crab blocking the defensive end back toward the center of the formation.

If the defensive end floats out along the line of scrimmage to string the play out, the back uses a Butt block to kick him out toward the sidelines. It is very important that he doesn't dive out or overextend at the defensive end. He must continue to fire-out at the defensive end until his nose is in the defensive end's numbers. If the defensive end keeps "feathering," the back simply runs at him until he slows down enough for contact to be made.

2. Kick-out Block: This block is nothing more than an isolation, or "Ice," block on the defensive end. The back uses an Out Butt technique with the near corner of the base of the defensive end's numbers as the aiming point. The back eventually tries to work his head to the inside. Movement off the line of scrimmage is still the major emphasis: if the defensive end stunts, or closes down quickly into the off-tackle hold, the back straight Butt blocks and drives him back and across the line of scrimmage. In this case, it is the ball carrier's job to be ready to slide to the outside off of the lead back's block if the blocking back is forced to block him to the inside.

3. Ice Block: This block is the use of a Butt block when isolating an inside linebacker. The technique is identical to a lineman's Butt block on a linebacker: the back must explode at the linebacker, but he must bring himself under control as he approaches the contact so as to not overextend or dive out at the linebacker. The back must attempt to square up if the linebacker is an inside linebacker. Again, it is of vital importance for the back not to attempt to blow through the linebacker until the nose actually is stuck into the linebacker's numbers.

4. Pass Block: The drop-back pass blocking always marries a back to a linebacker; thus, the back should never fear an overpowering rush from a defensive lineman. The backs utilize the same inside-out drop-back pass blocking techniques as the linemen. The only major exception is when a linebacker is on a heavy blitz which may be hard for the back to take on. If the linebacker is blasting in that fast, the back can fake the uncoiling action into the numbers and cut the blitzer down with a crab block just as contact is about to be made. The back must be careful to use this technique only when necessary since a smart linebacker can jump over or go around such a block if he can detect such a tendency early enough.

If the back has a Max blocking assignment, his role is simply to block the linebacker he is assigned if he blitzes and check for a seepage to his side or help out where necessary. Since the blocking emphasis is to draw the hands and arms of the pass rusher down, the back must fire-out and deliver a low Butt block; the aiming point is dead center at belt level.

5. Play Action Pass Blocking: This type of block is executed by utilizing an aggressive Butt block in the same fashion as the linemen. The head must be slid in front of the defender to prevent any penetration. If the defender can penetrate, the back must use a Cut-off block and kick the defender out toward the sidelines.

14

Developing a Receiver Corps for the Pro-Read Option Attack

The two running backs are just as important in their roles as receivers in the Pro-Read Option offense as the two ends and flanker. This chapter generally deals with pass receiving techniques for all receivers. Wide receiver and tight end play specific to those positions is so designated.

Very heavy emphasis must be placed on coaching the receivers. They must be convinced that all of their play is extremely valuable to the total play of the offense—run or pass. Careful examination of opposing teams on film shows that the play of the receivers is often the least effective part of the opposition's offense with regard to execution. Often the most lackadaisical play is seen by the receiver who is on a decoy cut, a blocking assignment or a clear-cut assignment. What better way to pick up a key on the offense!

Receiver play can easily become the most effective part of the offense. A wide receiver, by giving a total effort when running a flag cut fake on running play, can occupy up to three defensive players from the linebackers and deep backs. Even if such an occupation only lasts for a few split seconds, such a short duration may be the difference in springing a short power-play run into a long gainer. The same theory may be applied to a receiver's downfield blocking assignment: the extra effort in throwing a block on a free defender downfield after another receiver has caught the ball might well be the difference between a long gainer and a touchdown. As far as running decoy cuts, there are no such things in the passing offense. There may be prime receivers or assignments who try to occupy or clear cut zones. However, a receiver never knows, in line without reading and scanning concepts, when he may be the open receiver to whom the ball is thrown. Even if the receiver is the last receiver to whom the quarterback scans (a receiver who often does not receive the pass), there is no telling when spotters may notice that the secondary play is ignoring the cut of such a receiver. In such a case, the same pass pattern is used with the prime emphasis of throwing to that disregarded receiver.

Thus, receivers must be taught to believe that only a 100% effort on all assignments will do if they are to be an effective part of the passing and running game. Coaching staffs should accept nothing less.

A major focus in teaching receivers, and all the players on the entire offense for that matter, is to help them understand just how important their role is on each and every play. When a receiver is conceptually shown how important his particular role or assignment is in a play, he is just that much more apt to execute the assignment properly. When a receiver is shown, on a film or video-tape, how his failure to stay in the designated zone can allow a linebacker to cover two receivers, he can see that if he had stayed in his zone, either one or the other receivers would have been open to make the reception. Thus, the long-term average in running that particular pattern correctly over the course of the season would have given him a greater amount of receptions even though he may have been covered by that defender an equal number of times. Such a receiver easily can see and simply understand that if one defender can cover two receivers, neither receiver can be thrown to.

Conceptual teaching requires that the players understand the importance of their assignments if those assignments are to be meaningful to them. When a wide receiver is shown how his downfield block was the block that sprung the ball carrier loose for the touchdown, he is more apt and more highly motivated to execute that assignment each and every time. The receiver must be certain that "floating into the open area, hooking-up under the zone, flooding, clearing out," etc. are not just words used by the coach. Such terms must be highly pertinent teaching concepts that help the receiver, or player, to better understand the importance of his roles and assignments. In this manner, the individual player may achieve more successfully and add to the efficiency and effectiveness of the offensive and team play. There is a reason for everything: if players can understand why they are doing something, they can execute their assignments more effectively.

STANCE

The tight end's stance is a normal lineman's three-point stance. The wide receiver's stance is also a three-point stance; however, his legs are brought up under the body more than a running back's or lineman's three-point stance. From this stance, the wide receiver is better able to get off the mark into a sprinter's stride.

It does not matter which foot is staggered or which hand is placed on the ground; it is more important that the wide receiver is into a comfortable stance from which he can explode into the quickest release possible. Since the wide receivers don't wear large, bulky lineman's shoulder pads, they should not have much difficulty looking into the ball, even if their inside arm is the one they decide to place on the ground.

Looking into the ball is of great importance: the split end should see and move off of the movement of the ball on the center's snap; the flanker should see and move off of the movement of the ball on the center-quarterback exchange. Taking off on such ball movement is quicker than waiting for the sound signal since the split receiver is quite a distance from the quarterback. This is true more so on a windy day. Going on ball movement also cuts down on wide receiver off sides penalties.

TAKE-OFF AND RELEASE

The main emphasis of the release is the sprinter type of release of the wide receivers. A main theory of the passing game is for wide receivers to get off the line of scrimmage as quickly as possible. Such a release forces the deep backs to loosen and create a deeper and larger open area between the deep backs and the linebackers. Initially, the wide receiver explodes off the line of scrimmage using the step technique: the receiver steps out as quickly as possible with his back foot. The first two steps are shorter steps, helping the receiver to get an explosive start. In the burst off the line of scrimmage, it is again important to keep the elbows in tight to the body. This helps the receiver to keep a low center of gravity as he gradually begins to stride out and prevent the receiver from standing up and slowing himself down.

The tight end releases to the outside a greater percentage of the time in the Drop-Back Passing Series. He also uses the step technique by firing out toward the sidelines on approximately a 60° angle. When the tight end is on a straight ahead release, he often becomes entangled in jamming techniques from a linebacker and the defensive end. When this occurs, the tight end can utilize a few different techniques in his efforts to fight free to release from the line of scrimmage: the most desired type of release in this situation is just to explode off the line of scrimmage as quickly as possible so that the jam of the defense is ineffective. Basically, the tight end tries to catch the defensive players by surprise by "burning" past them before they can jam effectively.

If the tight end is getting jammed from two sides, or "sandwiched," but still finds daylight between the two defensive players, he can utilize a dropped shoulder technique in which the tight end drops his outside shoulder, turns the trunk of his body perpendicular to the line of scrimmage and rips up through the defensive jam by driving his shoulder up and through the defenders.

The slam and release is one of the most effective tight end releases. The tight end simply slam blocks the jamming defensive player for one quick count, faking the block, and releases into his pass cut. This release is extremely effective, for it often gives the defender a run key in which he tries to rid the tight end as quickly as possible to play the run.

If the tight end is getting slammed heavily on his release, he can utilize a spin-off technique as a change of pace, called a "change-of-pace" release since it is not used as a steady diet. It is too slow to be effective in the pass game if used constantly; however, if the tight end is being stymied in his attempt to release from the line of scrimmage, the spin-off technique can help to get him free.

The spin-off release simply sees the tight end roll opposite or into the pressure of the jam technique. The tight end plants the foot closest to the pressure and spins out and around the defensive player. When the tight end spins out, he must roll off the defensive player by arching his back and actually rolling off the body of the defensive player tightly. This helps the tight end release upfield quickly and prevents the defensive player from being able to react back to the spin-out and continue to jam.

If the wide receivers are being jammed, they should utilize speed and faking to get into their release. Such jamming usually takes the form of a bump-and-run type of play. When such a technique is used, the wide receivers should use a quick head and eye fake to one side or the other, while they explode off the line of scrimmage to the opposite side of the defender. The head and eye fake is often just enough to freeze the defender long enough for the receivers' quick bursts to get by him. A variation of this technique is to take a quick "jigger" step in the direction of the head and eye fake. If the wide receiver is being heavily jammed, he could utilize the spin-off technique; however, this is not preferred due to the slowing down effect it has on the receiver.

It is important that on all jamming techniques by the defense, the receiver must pump his arms and elbows hard to prevent any holding techniques. If the receiver is being held, he must actually chop down hard to break the defender's grasp. In addition, the receiver must accelerate quickly, taking long steps once he gets past a jamming defender. If the jamming technique is part of some type of man-to-man coverage, such long strides help the receiver to get by the defensive player greatly.

PASS CUTS AND FAKING

Chapters 4 and 5 discuss the use of pass cuts and their possible options; but how receivers run their cuts is of great importance. Each cut has a highly specific route and action that must be followed. The receiver does have options and the ability to float into the most open areas of the zone his cut puts him into. However, such flexibility requires strict discipline in execution. A receiver cannot float into an open area that is not in his assigned zone; his options only allow him either to bust deep, hook-up, or remain shallow. However, such options are dictated in regard to their execution. All receivers must execute as their assignments dictate if the coordination of the passing patterns are to be successful.

An important coaching point in the running of pass cuts is that the receiver must never slow down when running a deep cut (unless he is slowing down to adjust to an underthrown pass). Receivers do have options allowing them to float and hang under or in between various zone coverages. However, on deep post, flag and fly cuts, the receivers often have a tendency to slow down after a depth of twenty yards or more after releasing from the line of scrimmage. Perhaps the lack of confidence in the throwing ability of the quarterback, or just the feeling that the distance is too long for the quarterback to throw an accurate pass, is the rationale. Whatever the case may be, once a receiver slows his cut down, he breaks down the timing of the quarterback-receiver pass combination. More deep passes end up incomplete because of such a breakdown, rather than the inability of the quarterback to deliver the long pass.

When a receiver is utilizing a faking technique or changing his direction in some way, it is important that he brings his body under control, or "throttles down." The major emphasis in breaking away from a deep back or linebacker is not so much the fake, but the acceleration used to get away from that defender after the fake is made. Thus, receivers should set up their final break by veering to the off side of the receiver or giving a quick head and eye fake to the defender's offside. A heavy stepping and body fake is of little value if the receiver's body must again be brought under control giving the defender time to react back to the receiver's final break. Much like the receiver's releasing technique from a defensive jam, the faking or redirecting receiver must accelerate into fast, long strides to help him get away from the defender playing him.

Receivers must concentrate on making dull cuts, having sure footing and using gradual speed acceleration during wet conditions. A wet field and a wet day can be to their advantage offensively: they have just as great a chance of getting open on a wet field as they do on a dry field. While the receiver gradually accelerates, uses dull cuts and concentrates on sure footing, the defender has great difficulty backpedalling and tends to slip when the receiver makes his final cut and turns on the speed. Such a rainy day concept has proven to be correct many times in actual practice.

RECEIVING THE PASS

The basic teaching progression for receiving the ball is look the ball into your hands, catch the ball, tuck the ball under your armpit and run "North-South." Concentration is the major key: the receiver must look at the ball so intently that he must see it come into his hands. To help himself make the reception, the receiver must position himself in front of the path, or flight, of the ball so that his body is in direct line with the pass. The receiver must attempt to catch the ball at the highest point possible to prevent the defender from picking it off or knocking it away.

The receiver must *aggressively* go for the ball. His only thought must be that the pass is for him and that he *will* make the reception. If he cannot make the reception, he must make sure no one from the defense can. However, the philosophy is that anything a receiver can touch, he should catch. No matter what the situation, he *must* go for the ball. In addition, the receiver must never take his eyes off the ball. His responsibility is to catch the ball first, then run. A receiver cannot run with the ball unless he catches it.

When looking for the ball, the receiver must turn only his head and neck; turning the trunk of the body must only result from the outstretching of the hands and arms to make the reception. If the receiver runs his pattern with his upper body facing the quarterback, he only slows himself down and throws off the quarterback's timing when he makes the pass. By the same token, the receiver must never run with his hands up since this too only slows him down. The receiver's arms and hands only go up as the reception is about to be made.

As the reception is to be made, the receiver must relax his hands, arms and shoulders; they must not clench their hands if they are tight, for when the receiver opens his hands he will have an unnatural feeling that could throw off his feel for the ball. In addition, pre-game warm-ups should be extensive enough to get the receiver's hands loose. If a receiver has naturally tight hands, which a multitude of practice doesn't seem to correct, that player should take another position.

The general rule of "thumbs together" is used for a pass chest high or higher. When the pass is stomach high or lower, the little fingers should be together. The receiver must concentrate on a *soft* catch: the hands, fingers, arms and shoulders must act as "shock absorbers" that give with the forward motion of the ball as it makes contact with the fingers. The initial contact should be made with the fingertips, not the palms and heels of the hands or the body. (Again, the receiver must reach out and catch the ball at its highest point; he must not wait for the ball or allow the extra time necessary for a stomach, or basket type of catch.) Such a soft catch should not result in a slapping or thumping sound as the ball makes contact with the receiver's hands. If such a sound occurs, the receiver is catching the ball too stiffly. Another aid to making the reception is to make sure that the relaxed fingers are well spread, enabling them to surround the ball.

Another rule when making a reception is never to jump for the ball: this only causes the receiver to break his running stride and slow down. The only exceptions are when the receiver must lunge out to make a stab for a poorly thrown pass or when the receiver is in the end zone.

Tucking the ball away is vitally important. Great emphasis is placed in practice on "looking the ball into your hands" and then "looking the ball into your pit." Of course, the receiver should not "look the ball into his pit" in a game; but such heavy emphasis in practice during receiver drills helps to make such tucking away of the ball under the arm pit become automatic. Equally important is the emphasis on covering the tip of the ball with the fingers so that it is squeezed into the arm pit.

When a reception is made on an over-the-shoulder catch, it is important to emphasize tucking the ball immediately under the pit of the shoulder over which the ball is caught. A bad habit of many receivers, especially of right-handed receivers when making an over-the-shoulder catch over the left shoulder, is to try to bring the ball across the body to tuck it under the right armpit. Such crossbody maneuvering of the ball often results in a fumble if contact is made immediately after the reception. The receiver often does not see the tackler coming and is hit as he is trying to maneuver the ball across his body, resulting in the fumble.

Once the ball is tucked away, the receiver must run "North-South"; he must get upfield. Receivers should not cut back since statistics have shown that a receiver is more apt to lose yardage on such a technique. Of course, there are exceptions to this rule—if a split end with 9.4 speed runs like a jack-rabbit. However, he is the exception rather than the rule. In most cases, the consistent shorter gain should be taken by having the receiver break directly upfield and lower his shoulder once interference closes in on him. Such lowering the shoulder is often quite effective against the smaller deep back. As such contact is made the receiver must protect the ball by tightly securing under an armpit.

If the receiver has running room to maneuver in, he should break straight upfield and take a deep back straight on. The receiver or ball carrier now attempts to freeze the defender by running straight at him and breaking away sharply from him one way or the other once he is approximately two yards from the defender. Once the ball carrier makes his final cut, he must accelerate at top speed trying to break into full running strides to explode past the would-be tackler.

RECEIVER BLOCKING

One basic block is used for receivers on their downfield blocking assignments, a stalk, or slow, block. Since wide receivers probably are not the best blockers, their blocking technique is as simple as possible.

The stalk block simply attempts to fake a deep, fast pass cut release off of the line of scrimmage, has the receiver throttle down as he approaches the deep back to be blocked and attempts to interfere with the deep back's attempt to pursue to the ball. The block simply becomes a mirror technique in which the blocker tries to keep his body between the ball carrier and the deep back. The block does not attack the deep back or attempt to drive him out to one side or the other. Instead, the receiver just squares up in front of the deep back and maintains his position between the ball carrier and the deep back. Once the deep back commits himself to a side, the blocker simply rides him to the side he wants to go by walling him off.

Utilizing such a technique attempts to put the pressure on the deep back. The ball carrier helps set up the effectiveness of the block by running directly at the deep back, freezing him and forcing him to choose a side to pursue. Once the deep back does commit himself, the back simply breaks in the opposite direction. The receiver must develop the confidence that the deep back cannot run over him. Most deep backs are no bigger than the receivers; thus, they should not overpower the receivers. If the deep backs do try such an overpowering technique, the receiver should have an easy time tying the deep back long enough for the ball carrier to break to daylight.

The same technique is used for the wide receivers on their Max-Out or flag cut fakes when they loop back underneath in their attempts to get an inside-out position on the outside deep back. The only difference in this technique from the downfield block is that the receiver attempts to use his positioning to wall the defender off to the outside again by staying between the deep back and the ball carrier.

Once a reception is made by another receiver, all other receivers must become blockers: they must find someone to block. A receiver should fly across the field aggressively to knock down a deep back standing around, if the whistle has not yet been blown. Such a tactic may just well be the extra block needed to spring the ball carrier free for a touchdown. Even if the extra effort block does not accomplish such a goal, a few hard blocks on such a deep back standing around tends to make him wary of such action in the future. Split-second hesitations due to fear of such a block again may be the little extra needed to spring the ball carrier for that touchdown.

PRACTICE WITH PRESSURE

It is very important that all pass receiving drills be worked with as much pressure as possible. Catching a ball off of a pass cut with no one covering the receiver is an easy feat—too easy! In a game, that same receiver has a deep back or linebacker climbing all over him, bumping and slamming him and trying to jar the ball loose with a vicious tackle if a reception is made or as it is being made. A receiver cannot learn the necessary concentration required for his position unless he practices under such extensive pressure. Whether drilling one receiver at a time, skeleton pass scrimmage or a full passing scrimmage, coaches should try to play live on the receivers as much as possible.

15

Drills to Help Develop the
Pro-Read Option Attack

PRACTICE DRILLS

The actual tools that the coach works with in teaching and coaching any facet of the game are the practice drills. Whether it be a one-on-one pass blocking drill or an eleven-on-eleven passing scrimmage, the actual drills used are a major determining factor in just how good a team will understand what they are supposed to do and how well they can execute the offense. Therefore, the major philosophy of practice drills is to make them as game-like as possible. The first place to look for drills is not in a football drill book; instead, look to the offensive playbook. Look at the skills of the offense that need to be taught and then proceed to break down the actual play of the offense into game-like drills.

The use of game-like drills helps to avoid the use of artificial drills that are more concerned with executing that particular drill than with the execution of the drill as a part of the offense. Constantly ask the following questions: "What part of the offense is the drill teaching?" "Can a necessary drill be adapted to a particular part of the offense?" Instead of a trap drill with guards pulling out to trap a defensive tackle, the trap drill becomes a Blue, Counter Right drill, including all interior linemen from tackle to tackle and the offensive backfield. In this manner the trapping guard practices his trap action in its entirety—stance, count, pulling technique and trap block. At the same time, the line is practicing its complete

196

action for the downblocking technique. The backfield gets to practice its counter action off of the trapping action, and the entire unit gets to practice its individual skills versus a situation which highly simulates a live game action. By varying the bags and bagholders alignments to simulate the defense, a further game-like situation is created.

The progression of drills requires oral explanation, a walk-through version of the drill into a full-scale live action of the drill. Basically, such a progression teaches, explains and demonstrates. Specific aims for large-scale drills may be discussed or simulated on an overhead projector during the pre-practice meeting; all drills are short with an emphasis on sharp execution. The coaches must be sure there is a maximum of practice and a minimum of talk, called "coaching on the run." Comments should be made to an individual player after his drill performance is over as he goes to the end of the line or back to the huddle. If need be, the coach must pull the player out of the drill and replace him with another player. The drill must continue without interference. Of course, the coach might stop the drill to show how one particular player's performance is indicative of a problem a majority of other players are having.

"Correct practice" is another common phrase used in coaching techniques. Players should not be allowed to go through the motions; correct practice demands concentration. If they are not improving, they are falling behind. Short drills emphasize sharpness and concise practice to set a practice tempo full of spirit, desire and morale. The goal is quality of performance, not quantity: the consolidation of learning takes place from repetition through short, daily periods. All offensive drill execution is begun by a starting signal count and ended on a whistle. Such action greatly helps the take-off, preventing offside penalties and carrying out their assignments until the whistle is blown. It is very important that it becomes second nature to continue blocking and running until the whistle blows. Great second effort is produced through this coaching technique; it eliminates players from standing around when they could be hustling to make a second block through extra effort. Initial effort is not good enough; blasting a defensive tackle off the line of scrimmage is not enough; but continued driving of that tackle into the linebacker area might be the extra effort needed to tie up a linebacker's pursuit preventing him from getting to the ball carrier.

It is important that all drills be realistic in that they enable the players to meet definite goals and have the ability to meet success. Drills must never be so complex that the players have to concentrate on the drill and not the skills being practiced; yet, the drills always must be challenging and motivating. There should be allowance for progression in the drills so that the player may work from the simple to the complex in his skill development.

Drills should also be as enjoyable as possible. If there is some way the drills can enable the players to have fun while working hard, it should be done. Competition is always an excellent means of providing such fun and helping to motivate spirited practice. Pitting one player against another in a best-of-five series or an offensive pass scrimmage against a defense are excellent ways to produce such fun-type situations. A degree of variety also helps to make practice less of a drudgery; however, too many drills to accomplish the same goals only waste time.

The coach must be sure that he can watch all that goes on, and he must always be in position to see the total execution of the drill. The coach should have a comment after every attempt—good or bad, but his tone should always be positive. Incorrect performance should be corrected in a tone that gives the player confidence that if he takes certain measures to correct his performance, he can get the job done. Yelling or shouting at a player's incorrect performance only discourages further efforts through its demoralizing effect: he already knows he performed wrong; the coach must help show him why so he can correct himself.

Strong criticism in a negative fashion, however, does have its place. A lackadaisical attitude or lack of concentration cannot be tolerated. Neither can a player's "goofing" off or loafing. Incorrect performance can be understood, lack of effort, physically or mentally, cannot.

The following drills are examples of some of the game-like drills for individual position skills. Unit and team drills are not shown since they are simply breakdowns of large or even whole parts of this offense into drills. Thus, for a team drill practice the passing game with an eleven-on-eleven passing scrimmage; have a unit drill of the interior line and the backfield working on the counter series with its trapping action with one or two of the quarterbacks while the receivers work on their passing patterns with the rest of the quarterbacks.

LINE DRILLS

Heavy emphasis is placed on individual one-on-one blocking in individual line drills, shown in Diagrams 15-1 through 15-4. Such emphasis stems from the belief that one-on-one blocking is the core or base from which all offensive line play stems: trapping, pulling, cross blocking, etc. are all based on the ability of the individual to one-on-one block.

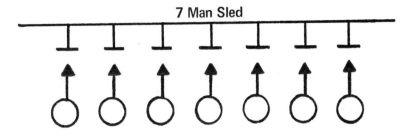

Diagram 15-1
Take-Off Drill

Drill
1. Fire out on snap count.
2. Deliver proper butt block.
3. Follow through until whistle.

Emphasis
1. Explosive take-off on snap count.
2. Maximum drive upon contact.
3. Maximum follow-through with good base and arched back until whistle.

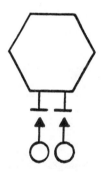

Diagram 15-2
Two-man Sled Drill

Drill
1. Fire out on snap count.
2. Deliver proper butt block.
3. Follow through until whistle.

Emphasis
1. Explosive take-off on snap count.
2. Maximum drive upon contact.
3. Maximum follow-through with good base and arched back until whistle.

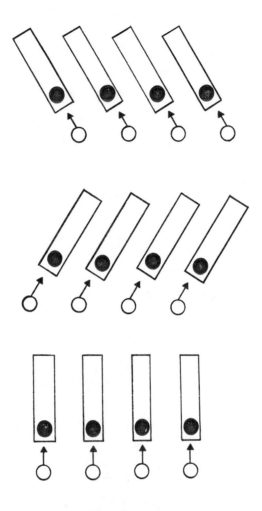

Diagram 15-3
Board Drills

Drill
1. Fire out on snap count.
2. Deliver proper butt block.
3. Follow through until whistle.

Emphasis
1. Explosive take-off on snap count.
2. Maximum drive upon contact with dummie.
3. Maximum follow-through with good base and arched back until dummie is driven off the board and whistle is blown.

Diagram 15-4
Butt Pass Blocking Drill

Drill
1. Drop back into pass blocking stance on snap count.
2. Deliver proper pass blocking technique to rusher.
3. Recoil into pass blocking stance.
4. Repeat until whistle is blown.

Emphasis
1. Proper pass blocking stance setup.
2. Explosive delivery of butt block into rusher from good base and with an arched back.
3. Quick recoil into proper pass blocking stance.

BACKFIELD DRILLS

The individual backfield drills practice the running skills of receiving handoffs, balance, handling the ball, shedding tacklers and blasting through tacklers to drive for extra yardage. These ten drills, shown in Diagrams 15-5 to 15-14, actually are run in a series of two minutes each. The series was developed from a similar series used by the coaching staff of Coach Cal Stohl while at Wake Forest University, as discussed by his assistant coach Tom Moore.

Although the major emphasis of individual backfield drills is ball carrying, some of the drills with blocking and pass receiving drills may be substituted. One day five running drills may be used and ten minutes spent on blocking drills. The next offensive practice may utilize the other five individual backfield drills and spend the other ten minutes on pass receiving drills.

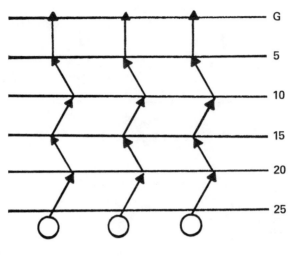

Diagram 15-5
Stumble Drill

Drill
1. Tuck ball under right arm and run to next yard line stripe.
2. Touch yard marker with left palm.
3. Regain balance, switch ball to under left arm and run to next yard line stripe.
4. Touch yard marker with right palm and again regain balance.
5. Repeat the set once more and reform the lines.

Emphasis
1. Make sure ball carrier touches ground with palm of hand forcing him to stumble.
2. As ball carrier stumbles, he must buck head up, stick out his chest, arch his back and pump his knees to regain his balance.
3. As the ball carrier switches the ball to the opposite arm, he must be sure to tuck it under his arm pit with his fingertips over the end of the ball.

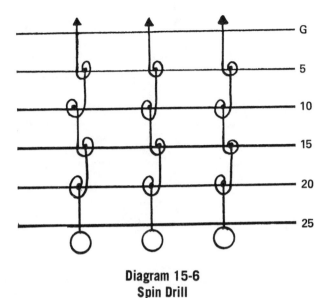

Diagram 15-6
Spin Drill

Drill
1. Tuck ball under right arm and run to the next yard line stripe.
2. Place left hand on the yard marker.
3. Spin (run) counter-clockwise around the hand placed on the ground.
4. Regain balance, switch ball to under left arm and run to next yard line stripe.
5. Place right hand on yard marker and spin clockwise.
6. Regain balance and repeat the set once more and reform the lines.

Emphasis
1. Make sure ball carrier touches ground with palm of hand.
2. As ball carrier runs around his hand, he must be sure not to get his feet tangled.
3. Ball carrier must utilize same skills required in Stumble Drill to regain balance, switch ball to under opposite arm and secure the ball under the arm.

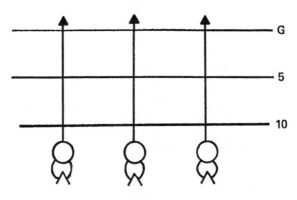

Diagram 15-7
Drag Drill

Drill
1. Ball carrier secures the ball in front of him with both arms clasping the ball.
2. A second ball carrier grasps the ball carrier around the waist as if making a tackle.
3. The ball carrier simulates driving into the end zone dragging the tackler for ten yards.
4. The ball carriers switch by coming back the opposite way.
5. Both ball carriers repeat the drill.

Emphasis
1. The ball carrier, simulating the tackler, tries to act as difficult an obstacle for the ball carrier as possible.
2. The ball carrier must secure the ball firmly and drive into the end zone by maintaining proper body lean, high knee pumping action and a proper spread of the feet to maintain a balanced based.

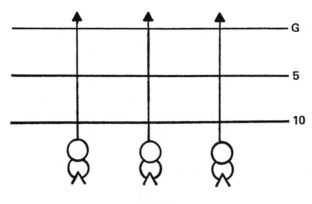

Diagram 15-8
Carry Drill

Drill
1. The Carry Drill is run in the exact same manner as the Drag Drill except that the ball carrier has the simulating tackle draped over his shoulder as if the tackler jumped on his back.

Emphasis
1. Same as Drag Drill.

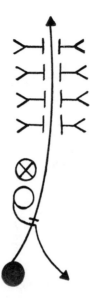

Diagram 15-9
Gauntlet Drill

Drill
1. Extra ball carriers form two lines a yard and a half across from one another with a yard spacing between each man. Each holds an air bag.
2. The bag holders slam the ball carrier high and low to try to knock him off balance or cause him to fumble.
3. The ball carrier drives through the gauntlet as fast and as powerfully as possible after taking a handoff from the quarterback.

Emphasis
1. Bag holders must vary the slams of the air bags high and low in trying to force the ball carrier to lose his balance.
2. If the ball is held loosely, the bag holders should try to jar it loose.
3. The ball carrier must secure the ball in front of him with both arms clasping the ball.
4. The ball carrier must drive up and through the gauntlet by arching his back. He must also be sure to pump his knees high to help him maintain his balance.

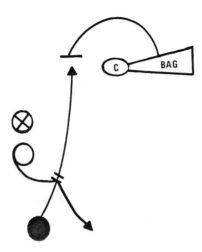

Diagram 15-10
Boomer Drill

Drill
1. Ball carrier takes handoff from quarterback and blasts through the swinging dummie that is trying to knock him off stride.
2. The coach swings a large bag at the ball carrier to try to knock him down or off balance.

Emphasis
1. The coach must slam the ball carrier with varied high and low blows.
2. The ball carrier must carry out proper techniques for securing ball with two arms, blasting up and through the bag with high knee pump.
3. Coach must be sure ball carrier does not close eyes or shy away from the hit of the bag.

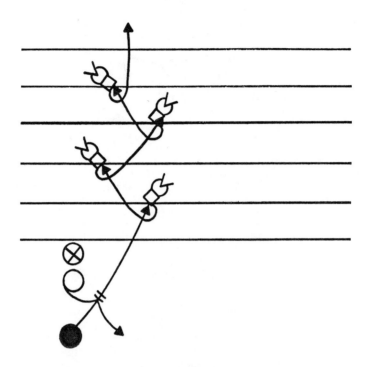

Diagram 15-11
Burma Road Drill

Drill
1. Ball carrier takes handoff from quarterback and attacks right bag with left shoulder. The dummies are supported by holders.
2. Ball carrier spins off bag to inside.
3. Ball carrier attacks next bag to left with right shoulder and again spins to inside.
4. Ball carrier repeats the set once more.

Emphasis
1. Ball carrier must use proper shoulder butting technique by driving up and through the dummie.
2. The ball carrier spins off the bag tightly by arching the back against the dummie to enable the ball carrier to get upfield quickly.
3. The ball carrier must be careful not to get his feet tangled up.

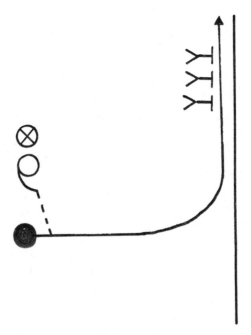

Diagram 15-12
Sideline Drill

Drill
1. Ball carrier takes toss pitch from quarterback and breaks up the sidelines simulating an end sweep.
2. Extra ball carriers hold air bags two yards from the sideline.
3. The ball carrier tucks the ball under his outside arm and uses inside shoulder to blast up and through the air bag.
4. The bag holders jam the ball carrier with varied blows trying to knock the ball carrier out of bounds.

Emphasis
1. Bag holders must vary the slams of the air bags high and low in trying to force the ball carrier out of bounds. Their position is two yards from the sideline.
2. The ball carrier must secure the ball underneath his outside arm.
3. The ball carrier must drive up and through the air bags by arching his back, slamming up and through the air bags with the free shoulder and using the forearm left to help shed the air bags.
4. The ball carrier must be sure to pump his knees high to help him maintain his balance.

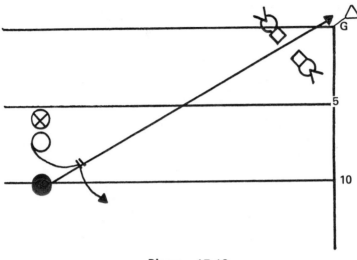

Diagram 15-13
Flag Drill

Drill
1. Two dummies are placed at the flag—one two yards straight out on a 45° angle and the other about a yard and a half from the goal line. The dummies are held by extra ball carriers approximately a yard apart.
2. The dummie holders must jam the ball carrier as hard as possible to prevent him from getting into the end zone.
3. The ball carrier must utilize his proper blast through driving technique to get into the end zone after taking his handoff from the quarterback.

Emphasis
1. The dummie holders must jam the ball carrier as hard as possible to prevent the ball carrier from getting into the end zone.
2. The ball carrier must secure the ball in front of him with both arms clasping the ball.
3. The ball carrier must drive up and through the dummies by arching his back. He must also be sure to pump his knees high to help him maintain his balance.
4. The ball carrier's aiming point is slightly inside of the flag.

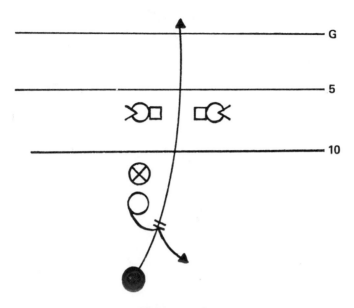

Diagram 15-14
Seven Yard Line Drill

Drill
1. Drill is set up similarly to the Flag Drill except the bags are set up on the seven-yard line.
2. The ball carrier, after taking the handoff from the quarterback, must blast through the bags and retain enough balance to get into the end zone.
3. Two extra ball carriers hold the dummies and jam the ball carrier to prevent forward motion.

Emphasis
1. The drill emphasizes skills similar to the gauntlet drill. The ball carrier must secure the ball in front of him with both arms clasping the ball.
2. The ball carrier must drive up and through the dummies by arching his back. He must also be sure to pump his knees high to help him maintain his balance.
3. An occasional signal by the coach will be given so the dummie holders fake a jam by not hitting him with the dummies at all. This is done to see if the ball carrier is overextending himself causing him to go directly to the ground.

RECEIVER DRILLS

All receiver drills are developed from pass cuts from the Drop-Back Passing Series. In this manner, receivers can practice their receiving skills while also practicing their cuts. These drills are shown in Diagrams 15-15 through 15-18.

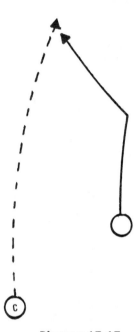

Diagram 15-15
Blind Catch Drill

Drill
1. Receiver runs a post cut (or any other designated deep cut).
2. The coach throws a deep pass in front of, behind, over or under the receiver.
3. When the ball is approximately over the receiver's head, the coach yells "ball."
4. The receiver then looks up and reaches to the ball.

Emphasis
1. The coach must vary the throw so the receiver learns to readjust to a poorly thrown pass.
2. The receiver must not look up for the ball until the signal is given and must run his cut at full speed just as he would in a game.

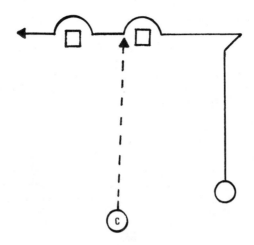

Diagram 15-16
Double Hop Drill

Drill
1. Receiver runs across cut (or any other designated short cut).
2. The receiver, as he is running across the field, must hop over the first bag, receive the pass, and hop over the second bag.
3. The coach must time the pass so the receiver can catch the ball sometime between his first and second straddle over the two bags.

Emphasis
1. Receiver must learn to concentrate on the ball despite interference.
2. Coach must vary the throw to cause foot coordination problems for the receiver.

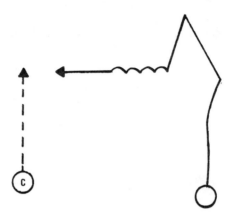

Diagram 15-17
Dive Drill

Drill
1. Receiver runs an across cut (or any other designated short cut).
2. The coach throws a pass that forces the receiver to extend his body to make a diving catch.
3. Receiver must fully extend his body to catch the ball.

Emphasis
1. The receiver must run at top speed.
2. The coach should vary the wide pass high and low.
3. The receiver must learn to maintain concentration even though he is forced to dive, lunge or jump for the ball.
4. The receiver must learn to grasp the ball firmly as he makes contact with the ground so he maintains the reception.
5. If the ball is close to the ground, he must get his hands under the ball so he scoops it before it hits the ground so he doesn't trap it.

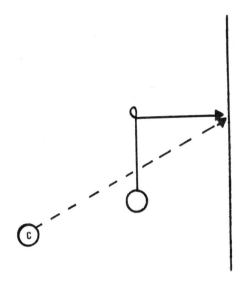

Diagram 15-18
Out-Of-Bounds Drill

Drill
1. Receiver runs a designated out cut.
2. Coach throws a pass that forces reception to be made at sidelines.
3. Receiver must make reception and keep one foot inbounds.
Emphasis
1. The coach must vary the types of passes high and low.
2. The receiver must both concentrate on the ball and learn to "feel" the sideline.
3. The receiver must learn to come down with one foot inbounds or drag one foot on the ground as he makes the reception.

QUARTERBACK DRILLS

Although the quarterbacks work with the receivers and backs quite often during individual drills so they can practice handoffs, pitching, faking, etc., there are specific individual quarterback drills for them to practice. Shown in Diagrams 15-19 through 15-22, they are basically passing drills.

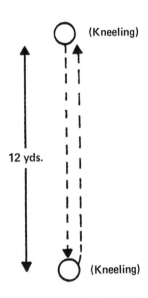

Diagram 15-19
Kneeling Pass Drill

Drill
1. Two quarterbacks kneel on the ground facing one another at a distance of twelve yards. The knee corresponding to the throwing is placed on the ground.
2. The quarterbacks use their proper passing techniques to practice passing the ball with proper "zip" at the outstretched hands of the opposite quarterback which act as a target.

Emphasis
1. Normal "throwing darts" type of emphasis is placed on the technique.
2. Since stepping into the pass is not possible, leading with the chest and proper arm and shoulder follow-through is emphasized.

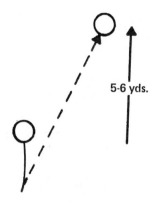

Diagram 15-20
Mike Dump Drill

Drill

1. Quarterback takes normal drop-back action setup.
2. On second and third steps, the quarterback throws ''Mike-Hot'' dump passes to another quarterback standing approximately five to six yards deep slightly inside of the tight end's alignment.
3. The quarterback catching the ball gives the passing quarterback a target by holding his hands up approximately chest high. The quarterbacks alternate the passing each time.

Emphasis

1. The quarterback must vary his dump passes off the second and third drop-back step.
2. The quarterback must be sure to gather himself quickly by ''standing tall'' so that he can raise up on the balls of his feet to get proper ''zip'' on the ball.
3. The quarterback must follow through heavily with his arm action to get such ''zip'' on the ball.

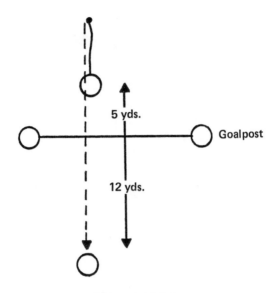

Diagram 15-21
Goalpost Passing Drill

Drill
1. Two quarterbacks face one another on opposite sides of the goalpost.
2. The two quarterbacks alternate passing and catching by having one quarterback set up as a target 12 yards from the goalposts with hands up at chest high level. The passing quarterback sets up in a normal snap stance with the ball in his hands approximately 5 yards from the goalpost.
3. The passing quarterback takes his normal eight-step drop back and passes to the target by throwing over the goalpost.
4. The quarterbacks alternate on each pass.
Emphasis
1. Proper drop-back and setup technique.
2. Proper "dart type" passing technique.
3. Ball must go over posts (simulating passing over defensive lineman's arms). Yet, the pass must not be floated over the goalposts. It must be a sharp pass that crosses the goalpost as closely as possible while aiming for the target.

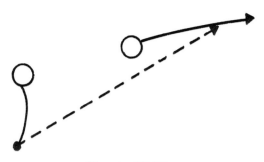

Diagram 15-22
Blood Dump Drill

Drill
1. Quarterback takes his normal drop-back action setup.
2. On the fourth step the quarterback opens up to the sidelines on his setup and throws a ''Blood-Hot'' dump pass.
3. The opposite quarterback simulates a tight end on a shute cut release and receives the dump pass.
4. The quarterbacks alternate their passing each time.

Emphasis
1. The quarterback must gather himself quickly as he sets up on his fourth step to throw the dump pass.
2. Since the pass is made quickly, the quarterback must learn to develop a quick release while still stepping into the pass and properly following through.

Index